# CULTURE SMART!
# NETHERLANDS

Sheryl Buckland

·K·U·P·E·R·A·R·D·

ISBN 978 1 85733 312 1
This book is also available as an e-book: eISBN 978 1 85733 587 3

British Library Cataloguing in Publication Data
A CIP catalogue entry for this book is available from the British Library

Copyright © 2003 Kuperard
**Revised 2008; fourth printing 2011**

First published in Great Britain 2003
by Kuperard, an imprint of Bravo Ltd
59 Hutton Grove, London N12 8DS
Tel: +44 (0) 20 8446 2440   Fax: +44 (0) 20 8446 2441
www.culturesmart.co.uk
Inquiries: sales@kuperard.co.uk

Distributed in the United States and Canada
by Random House Distribution Services
1745 Broadway, New York, NY 10019
Tel: +1 (212) 572-2844   Fax: +1 (212) 572-4961
Inquiries: csorders@randomhouse.com

Series Editor  Geoffrey Chesler
Design  Bobby Birchall

Printed in Malaysia

Cover image: Windmills and water.
*iStockphoto/Floris Sloof*

# About the Author

SHERYL BUCKLAND is an English management trainer and consultant who has worked for public and private organizations in Britain and the Netherlands. A member of the British Chartered Institute of Personnel Development, she holds a BA (Hons.) degree in English and European Thought and Literature and an MA in Education. In 1995 she moved with her husband to the Netherlands and immersed herself in Dutch culture, conducting research on cultural acclimatization, the role of language teachers, and child development. During this time, she has also worked as an Associate Lecturer for the British Open University Business School, and conducted intercultural training for a major Anglo-Dutch corporation.

The Culture Smart! series is continuing to expand.
For further information and latest titles visit
**www.culturesmartguides.com**

The publishers would like to thank **CultureSmart!**Consulting for its help in researching and developing the concept for this series.

**CultureSmart!**Consulting creates tailor-made seminars and consultancy programs to meet a wide range of corporate, public-sector, and individual needs. Whether delivering courses on multicultural team building in the USA, preparing Chinese engineers for a posting in Europe, training call-center staff in India, or raising the awareness of police forces to the needs of diverse ethnic communities, it provides essential, practical, and powerful skills worldwide to an increasingly international workforce.

For details, visit www.culturesmartconsulting.com

**CultureSmart!**Consulting and **CultureSmart!** guides have both contributed to and featured regularly in the weekly travel program "Fast Track" on BBC World TV.

# contents

# contents

# Map of the Netherlands

# introduction
introduction

*Culture Smart! Netherlands* is written for those travelers who want to get to the heart of the country. It describes the main features of Dutch society and culture and offers insights and practical advice on what to expect and how to behave in different circumstances.

In painting this picture it has been necessary to use a broad brush. Generalizations, of course, have their limitations. For every description of a "typical Dutch person in a typical situation" there will be somebody who behaves quite differently. However, over the centuries certain national characteristics have evolved. The Dutch are renowned for their organizational skills and their commercial acumen. They are known for being hospitable, friendly, pragmatic, tolerant, fair-minded, and just. They are famous for their struggle to control the sea that constantly threatens to flood their land, and their hydraulic engineers are highly regarded throughout the world. At the height of its power in the seventeenth century, this small seafaring nation led Europe and the world in cultural and scientific endeavor, and laid the foundations for the modern age.

The book covers different aspects of Dutch life. The chapters on social values and attitudes and on the way business is conducted offer psychological insights and practical advice that will help in your personal and professional dealings with Dutch people. Personal vignettes and case studies illustrate the general points. Other sections provide background information on geography, politics, and government. One of the most important of these is the brief historical outline—a people are their collective memory, and Dutch history and contemporary culture are closely intertwined.

There is also more general information—for instance on travel, accommodation, and festivals in the Netherlands. You can use the index or the extended contents pages to dip into sections that particularly interest you, or you can start at the beginning and work through from cover to cover.

*Culture Smart! Netherlands* introduces you to the inner life of the Dutch people and the subtle complexities of their culture. As the historian Simon Schama says in *The Embarrassment of Riches*: "But if there is one Dutch culture, there are many rooms within it . . . it can swim with variety yet remain coherent unto itself. And such puzzles divert. They can even instruct." Great riches await the visitor. Enjoy your reading!

# Key Facts

| | | |
|---|---|---|
| **Official Name** | The Kingdom of the Netherlands (Koninkrijk der Nederlanden) | |
| **Capital City** | Amsterdam | |
| **Main Cities** | The Hague, Rotterdam, Utrecht, and Maastricht. | |
| **Area** | 16,033 square miles (41,526 square kilometers) | Approx. the size of Massachusetts and Connecticut combined. |
| **Climate** | Temperate | |
| **Currency** | Euro—this currency was introduced on January 1, 2002. | |
| **Population** | 16.2 million | The most heavily populated country per square kilometer in Europe. |
| **Ethnic Makeup** | 83% Dutch, 17% other. | About 9% are of non-Western origin: Turks, Moroccans, Antilleans, Surinamese, and Indonesians. |
| **Family Makeup** | Av. family size: 4 to 5 people. | |
| **Language** | Dutch | English is the main foreign language taught in schools, and is widely understood. |
| **Religion** | 40% unaffiliated, 31% Roman Catholic, 21% Protestant, and 8% other (including 5% Muslim and 0.5% Hindu). | |

| | | |
|---|---|---|
| **Government** | The Netherlands is a constitutional monarchy. | The Monarch is head of state—currently Queen Beatrix. The Prime Minister is the head of government. There are twelve provinces. |
| **Dependent Areas** | Aruba and the Netherlands Antilles | |
| **Media** | The Dutch Broadcasting Association (*De Nederlandse Omroep Stichting*) coordinates broadcasting on national TV and radio. | There are a large number of national and regional newspapers and magazines. |
| **Media: English Language** | English-language daily newspapers (American and British) can be bought from all big railway stations, as well as from some newsdealers. | Several Dutch English-language publications cater to expatriates and businesspeople. See www.expatica.com for a daily summary of the Dutch news. |
| **Electricity** | 220 volts, 50 Hz | Two-pronged plugs used. Transformers needed for U.S. appliances and adapters for British appliances. |
| **Video/TV** | PAL B system | |
| **Internet Domain** | .nl | |
| **Telephone** | The country code for the Netherlands is 31. | To dial out, dial 00. Private companies may have special codes. |

# chapter one

# LAND & PEOPLE

The Netherlands is often referred to as Holland, which is actually the name of two of its twelve provinces. This small country on the northwestern seaboard of Europe occupies an area of 16,033 square miles (41,526 square kilometers). It is densely populated. The majority of the 16.2 million people who live there are concentrated in the west, especially within the *Randstad*—"Rim Town," or urban conglomeration—the irregularly shaped area lying between Amsterdam, The Hague, Rotterdam, and Utrecht. The areas of thinnest population are in the north of the country.

The Dutch have spent centuries battling against the sea, to keep it from flowing into and over low-lying parts of the land. This constant fight against the elements is said to have been a key influence in forming their general character, as well as particular aspects of Dutch society. While the water has been an enemy in some respects, it has been harnessed as an ally in others. A maritime nation, the Dutch set to sea early in their history to trade with other countries. The network of rivers and canals within the country has been used for transportation and as part of their defenses, and more recently for leisure activities.

The Netherlands has a mixed reputation abroad. Some people believe it to be a country where "anything goes" because of its liberal attitude toward soft drugs, prostitution, homosexuality, and matters such as euthanasia. While it is true that many Dutch laws are very liberal, this gives only a partial picture of attitudes in the country as a whole. Other people abroad focus on the Dutch reputation for tolerance, concern for justice, and respect for human rights. This, too, is an important element of Dutch culture, but again it belies the complexities of life in the Netherlands today.

## GEOGRAPHICAL OVERVIEW

The Netherlands is bounded to the north and west by the North Sea, to the east by Germany, and to the south by Belgium. It is about the size of Massachusetts and Connecticut together, or the area of the south of England. Situated at the mouths of three major European rivers, the Rhine, the Meuse or Maas, and the Scheldt, its name *Nederland* ("low land") refers to its low-lying nature. *Holland*, similarly, means "land in a hollow." Nearly a quarter of the country is below sea level, and much of the rest is at or just above it, which makes flooding along its 280-mile (425-kilometer) coastline the greatest natural hazard. The lowest point is at *Zuidplaspolder*—22 feet (6.7 meters) below sea level. There is a constant battle to keep nature under control and the sea at bay. Because of this the Dutch have excelled at hydraulic engineering. Dikes are used extensively to prevent flooding. The largest of these is the 20-mile (32-km) long *Afsluitdijk* (the "Closing Dike"), which was constructed in the early 1930s, joining the provinces of North Holland and Friesland via the road that runs along the top of it. The dike closed off the North Sea and turned part of the Zuiderzee into what is now a freshwater lake—the Ijsselmeer. The *Afsluitdijk* made it possible to drain parts of the Ijsselmeer and turn them into *polders* (land reclaimed from under the water). This reclaimed land now forms the province of Flevoland. The main delta area of the Netherlands forms the southwestern province of Zeeland. It is protected from flooding by an enormous complex of dams and bridges called the Delta

Works, built during the 1980s and 1990s, that combine to control the water level.

The landscape of the Netherlands is not totally flat and featureless, as many people expect it to be. There are distinct regional variations: sand dunes and lowland start by the sea in the west and north, leading to the wooded Utrecht *heuvelrug* (hilly ridge) in the center, and the sandy areas in the east of the country. North Brabant and the province of Gelderland contain most of the wooded countryside. There are also areas of heather-filled heath in Gelderland and in the province of Drenthe. Finally, there are the slightly higher hills in the southeastern province of Limburg, near the borders of Germany and Belgium. The highest point of the Netherlands is in this province, at Vaalserberg Hill, which is 1,053 feet (321 meters) above sea level. Each area has its own fauna and flora and there are nature reserves across the country.

To the north of the country are the Wadden Sea Islands ( *Waddeneilanden* ). The sea in this area is very shallow, and at low tide at certain times of the year it is possible to take a guided walk across the mudflats from the mainland to the islands at particular points (see Chapters 6 and 7).

If you are flying over the Netherlands, the two things that strike you are the amount of water and the regularity of the landscape. The Dutch like things to be neat, and this is evident in the regular

patchwork of fields, crisscrossed by waterways.
When you are at ground level, the changing quality
of the light is impressive. No wonder there have
been so many famous Dutch landscape painters.

Windmills were used to harness
the energy of the wind in order to
pump out water from the lowlands.
Many can still be seen, but the vast
majority are now simply a
charming tourist attraction.

**CLIMATE**
The climate is temperate. Generally the
summers are cool and the winters are mild, but
cold snaps can occur in January and February.
When the temperatures drop and the canals and
lakes freeze over, the Dutch get out their skates
and take to the ice. At these times, the skies are
a brilliant periwinkle blue, the sun shines, and
everybody has a great time in the open air.
People take hot-air balloon rides to enjoy the
marvelous views.

When you come to the Netherlands, bring
an umbrella and waterproof clothes. It can be
spring, summer, fall, or winter, but rain is a
part of every season. The Dutch make the best of
circumstances. At the slightest hint of sunshine,
tables and chairs will be out on the café terraces.

## THE DUTCH PEOPLE: A BRIEF HISTORY

In order to understand modern Dutch society, some knowledge of the past is necessary. What follows is a rough sketch of the major periods in Dutch history, highlighting some of the individuals who have influenced Dutch thinking.

### The Early Years

The earliest inhabitants of the Netherlands were hunter-gatherers who lived on the hills in the center of the country around 150,000 BCE. The last Ice Age drove them away and people did not return until around 9000 BCE. By 6000 BCE farmers were living on the banks of rivers and in the hills. At the end of the Bronze Age (between 1900 and 750 BCE) the southern part of the country was populated by Celts, and Germanic peoples occupied the north. During the Iron Age (from 750 BCE) people began to settle in the lower, more fertile areas. The threat of flooding was very high, so they constructed artificial hills (*terpen*) upon which to build their homes and farms.

### The Romans

Gradually the northern tribes drove the Celts further south. By the time Julius Caesar began his conquest of the Netherlands it was inhabited mainly by Germanic tribes—the Batavians in the regions around the large rivers, and the Frisians further north. The Romans controlled only the Celtic lands south of the Rhine from 57 BCE to 406 CE. They did not conquer the north, and their influence on the northern Germanic tribes was exerted largely through trade.

In spite of Roman efforts to control flooding with dams, the sea continually flooded the western part of the Netherlands. Gradually the area turned into a peat bog unfit for people to live in. At the same time, the northern borders were coming under attack. Unrest at the center of the Empire meant that troops were needed closer to home, and in 406 CE the Romans pulled back, abandoning their forts along the Rhine.

With the departure of the Romans, Germanic culture took hold. The Frisians extended southward, Saxon invaders settled in the east, and Franks overran the area south of the Rhine and the Maas. By the early sixth century, the Franks controlled Gaul (present-day France) and northern Italy. The Frankish king Clovis I converted to Christianity at the start of the sixth century. By the eighth century the Franks had imposed Christianity on almost all of the country.

### Charlemagne
In 800 Charlemagne, King of the Franks, was crowned Emperor of the Romans by Pope Leo III

in Rome. In the Netherlands he installed his counts or princes to administer justice and to organize the collection of taxes. They were also charged with the control of military matters. In return, they were given land and certain privileges. Gradually the power base of these nobles increased. When Charlemagne died in 814 the central authority of the Frankish Empire declined and many of the wealthiest regional nobles ruled practically independently.

From the ninth to the twelfth centuries the Netherlands was repeatedly partitioned in the divisions of the Holy Roman Empire, not falling clearly into either the French or the German kingdoms. From 850 onward, Viking raiders from Scandinavia took advantage of the situation. A few settled, but most withdrew in 892 when the harvest was so bad that richer pickings were to be had from raids on England. Viking raids ceased entirely by the beginning of the eleventh century.

## The Middle Ages

In 925, all of present-day Netherlands was incorporated into the Holy Roman Empire. Larger principalities were formed by consolidating some of the smaller counties. The feudal lords grew stronger and the territories that would later become the Dutch provinces began to be established.

By the fifteenth century a number of towns had become prosperous trading centers. Usually ruled by small groups of merchants, they effectively became self-governing republics. Some joined the Hanseatic League, an organization that protected the trading interests of leading North Sea and Baltic port cities. Citizens within the towns began to exert a strong influence over politics and economic affairs.

In the fifteenth century, all the Low Countries (today's Belgium, Netherlands, and Luxemburg) came under the rule of the dukes of Burgundy. In 1464 some of the regional assemblies tried to resist the centralization imposed  upon them by Philip the Good, Duke of Burgundy (1396–1467). They met in Bruges, and the "States-General' (*Staten-Generaal*), as the assembly was known, thereafter became a part of joint government in the regions.

### Religion and Revolt
The discovery of the New World shifted interest from the Mediterranean to countries on Europe's western seaboard, and during the sixteenth

century the Netherlands developed rapidly and grew in importance.

Protestantism found a ready audience among the strong-willed Dutch nobility and merchant class. The Dutch Humanist scholar Desiderius Erasmus (c. 1466–1536) had an enormous influence on the way that educated people throughout Europe thought about the teachings and practices of the Roman Catholic  Church. When the Augustinian monk Martin Luther (1483–1546) challenged the authority of the Church and instigated the Protestant Reformation, there followed a period of bitter religious wars. The exiled French reformer John Calvin (1509–64) established a form of lay theocracy in Geneva that would provide a model for "the most perfect school of Christ."

In 1530, the Habsburg ruler Charles V, King of Spain (who had been born in Ghent), was crowned Holy Roman Emperor. In the great political and religious upheaval of the times, he staunchly supported the Pope, and introduced the Inquisition to the Netherlands to deal with heretics. Many Dutch people were tortured and killed.

In 1555, Charles retired to a monastery and handed over the seventeen states of the Netherlands to his son, Philip II (1527–98). Philip believed in firm government. He chose several members of the largely Protestant Dutch nobility to act as his governors (*stadhouders*, placeholders) in the large provinces, but increasingly made decisions without consulting them. His rule of the Netherlands was high-handed, remote, and insensitive to local interests and traditions. He levied heavy taxes and restricted trade in the middle of an economic crisis, and was even more determined to suppress the Protestants than his father.

In spite of, or possibly because of, this, Protestantism took a stronger hold on the people, and the rigid beliefs of Calvinism became even more popular than Lutheranism. Trouble was brewing. When a group of Protestant nobles presented a "Request" for more lenient treatment in 1556, they were described by one Spanish counselor as "beggars," a name they immediately adopted. Soon after this, Calvinist and Anabaptist mobs stormed through Catholic churches in the Netherlands, destroying church treasures and works of art, to the cry of "Long live the Beggars."

William of Nassau, Prince of Orange (1533–84), was the Burgrave of Antwerp and *stadhouder* for Holland, Utrecht, and Zeeland. Increasingly alienated by Spain's policy of centralized rule and religious oppression, in 1567 he refused to renew his allegiance to Philip, and fled the country in the company of many Calvinists to lead the rebellion against Spain. Philip responded by sending an army to the Netherlands, headed by the ruthlessly effective Duke of Alba. The years that followed saw thousands of rebels killed.

### The "Sea Beggars"

William the Silent (as William became known) raised armies in Germany and made several attempts to free territory in the Netherlands from Spanish rule. Defeated on land, he continued the struggle at sea by means of the so-called "Sea Beggars" (*Watergeuzen*). These semi-pirates were Dutch patriots who raided ships carrying merchandise between Spain and the Netherlands, with cautious support from the English. William's aim was to unite the Dutch, Protestant and Catholic, against their common enemy. At first, many people in the Netherlands did not support him, but there was a change of heart when, in response to his losses, Philip levied even higher taxes, further reducing the political and economic power of both the wealthy burghers and the aristocracy. In 1572 the Sea Beggars captured the port of Brill, from which they established control over the entire Scheldt estuary and the approaches to Antwerp.

### The Republic of the North

In 1579 seven northern rebel provinces signed the Union of Utrecht, which is regarded as the foundation charter of the Dutch Republic. In the same year Philip's new governor, Alexander Farnese, reunited much of the Catholic south and east for Spain. In 1581 the northern provinces declared their independence, and William was elected *stadhouder* of the new Republic of the North (north of the river Rhine). In 1584 he was assassinated by a Catholic fanatic, hired by Spain. Under his son Maurice and Jan van Oldenbarneveldt, however, the rebels regained lost ground.

The conflict dragged on until 1648, when Spain finally acknowledged the sovereignty of the Republic of the North in the Treaty of Münster. It was agreed in principle that Catholic worship would be allowed in the Republic (although in practice *open* Catholic worship was not allowed and Catholicism was not formally recognized). The Catholic south remained loyal to Spain, and would later become Belgium. During the course of the revolt, as much as 10 percent of the population of the more highly developed south moved to the northern provinces.

### The Golden Age

During the seventeenth century, the Netherlands became one of the world's greatest trading nations.

It acquired a vast overseas empire through its power at sea, and Amsterdam overtook Antwerp as the center of international trade. As the economy thrived, so did cultural activity. This is the era of the great Dutch scholars, philosophers, jurists, bankers, engineers, and scientists. In 1625 the exiled Humanist Huig de Groot (Hugo Grotius) wrote *On the Law of War and Peace*, laying the foundations of international law. He also wrote about the freedom of the seas and international trade. Artists such as Rembrandt, Frans Hals, Steen, and Vermeer broke with "classicism" in painting and changed the way we view the world. The Netherlands became the powerhouse of change—exporting ideas, skills, technology, capital, and enterprise. In a real sense it propelled Europe into the modern age.

The economy of the Dutch Republic was given a huge boost by the formation of the great trading companies. The Dutch United East India Company (*Verenigde Oostindische Compagnie*, or VOC), founded in 1602, maintained its own fighting ships to defend its merchant vessels and its own army to protect its colonies and settlements. The Dutch West India Company was formed in 1621. It traded mainly in slaves who were brought from Africa to America to work on

the new plantations. Colonies
were established in the
Dutch East Indies
(Indonesia), Suriname (as
Dutch Guiana, in the north
of South America), the
Netherlands Antilles in the
Caribbean, and at the Cape of Good
Hope, on the southern tip of Africa. During the
early 1600s there was a fierce struggle for
economic supremacy between the Netherlands
and England, which culminated in the wars of
1652–4 and 1664–7.

### New York and the Dutch

In 1609 Henry Hudson, the English explorer
commissioned by the Dutch East India Company
to look for a western passage to India, sailed into
New York Bay and up the Hudson River. The
Netherlands claimed the territory, and established
a colony and trading post at New Amsterdam,
later managed by the Dutch West India Company.
New Amsterdam was lost to Britain in 1664 in the
course of the second Anglo-Dutch War, when it
was exchanged for Suriname, and was
subsequently christened New York in honor of the
Duke of York.

After the treaty with Spain in 1648, there was a
struggle for political power within the Dutch

Republic between the *Stadhouder*, William II, and the regents of the individual States of the Republic. William, who was married to Mary Stuart, the daughter of Charles II of England, wanted to support the royalist cause in the English Civil War. The States did not want to be involved—it was expensive and not good for trade. Later on, in 1677, William III married another Mary Stuart, James II's daughter. He was offered the English throne in 1689 by the Whig opponents of James, who feared that he was about to reintroduce Roman Catholicism. As both *Stadhouder* and King of England William was able to harmonize the colonial and commercial policies of the two countries. In 1674 the office of *Stadhouder* became hereditary in the Orange family. William III died in 1702.

### French Rule

From 1689 to 1713, the Dutch and the English formed a coalition against the ambitions of Louis XIV of France. The wars against France, which ended with the signing of the Treaty of Utrecht in 1713, took a heavy toll on Dutch finances. As a result England came to rule the trade routes formerly dominated by the Dutch, and became the leading commercial and industrial power. Exhausted, the Netherlands went into decline.

When William IV died in 1751 democratic ideas were spreading through the country. A group named the Patriots called for democratic constitutional reforms and limitations to the *Stadhouder*'s powers. The Patriots were inspired by the colonial rebellion in America. Their more radical members drew up a constitution based upon the American Declaration of Independence.

William V defeated the Patriots in the 1780s with the help of his brother-in-law, the King of Prussia. However, they returned in 1795 with the French Revolutionary army and were welcomed by the populace. William went into exile. The radicals renamed the Dutch Republic the Batavian Republic. They instituted the separation of Church and State, guaranteed freedom of worship, and granted all religions legal equality.

In 1806 Napoleon made his brother Louis Bonaparte King, transforming the Batavian Republic into the Kingdom of Holland. Louis established his court in Amsterdam, which became the capital. He was actually a rather benevolent ruler, who started to keep some of the taxes for himself and allowed the Dutch to contravene some of the Imperial orders. He was removed from his position in 1810. However, Napoleon's defeat at Leipzig in 1813 spelled the collapse of his power outside France, and he withdrew his troops from the Netherlands. Supporters of the House of Orange took power, declared a constitutional monarchy, and invited the heir to the House of Orange (the son of William V) back to the country. He was crowned King William I in 1814.

### Independence

In the post-Napoleonic settlement at the Congress of Vienna in 1815, the seventeen states of the former "Seventeen United Netherlands" were reunited under the restored House of Orange. They did not stay united for long. After two and a half centuries of separation the differences in religion, culture, language, politics, and economics had become far too wide. In 1830, the dissatisfied Southerners seceded—with British and French help—and formed the independent state of Belgium. In 1839, after several years of negotiation, William finally confirmed the separation of Belgium and the northern Netherlands became known as the Kingdom of the Netherlands.

During his reign, William did much to improve the economy of the Netherlands and to try to create a unified Dutch culture. In 1840, he abdicated in order to marry a Belgian Roman Catholic countess. He was succeeded by his son, William II, and died just three years later.

In 1848, in order to secure his position in the face of the rising tide of liberalism within Europe, William II agreed to constitutional changes that increased parliamentary democracy and subordinated the monarchy to a directly elected government. This still forms the basis of Dutch government today. On William's death in 1849 the throne passed to his son, William III.

The 1870s saw a rise in the fortunes of the Netherlands. New industries thrived and the country began to reap the benefits of industrial progress. The Dutch colonial empire in the East was strengthened. Increased prosperity had a positive effect upon culture and the arts, too.

William III died in 1890 and his daughter Wilhelmina, who was only ten years old at the time, ascended to the throne. The Netherlands entered the twentieth century on a high note. Although it was no longer the force in Europe that it had been, there was pride in the developments at home and in its renewed status as a trading nation.

**"Pillarization"** (*Verzuiling*)
This term describes a peculiarly Dutch arrangement—the segregation of society along political and religious lines. In the late nineteenth century Dutch society split into

distinct sections or communities. Each of these groups (or "pillars") had its own religion, schools, media, political party, and even sports clubs. Within each pillar there were different social levels—workers and professional classes, religious and political leaders—although the contribution of *all* individuals to the success of the community was acknowledged.

The idea was to "live apart together." The sections of society were separate, but seen as contributing to the common interest of the country as a whole. Imagine a classical building with a roof held up by separate columns, using their combined strength to support it. For this system to work, political leaders had to seek a consensus in order to make a decision.

### World War II (1939–45)

The Netherlands had remained neutral during World War I, and was determined to stay out of World War II. The majority of the population was pacifist, there was no army to speak of, and a great deal of its trade was with Germany. However, Germany invaded the Netherlands on May 10, 1940. Rotterdam was heavily bombed. Within five days the Dutch army was overwhelmed. The Dutch Resistance movement went underground, and Queen Wilhelmina rallied the people from London by broadcasting over the BBC.

In spite of the noble efforts of ordinary Dutch families to hide them, 100,000 Jews were deported from the Netherlands and killed in concentration camps. Dutch men were also taken to work in Germany. Many people suffered extreme deprivation, especially in the last year of the war when food was scarce and the winter was hard. The Allied forces liberated the Netherlands on April 29, 1945, and the war ended on May 5.

### The Colonies

The Dutch East Indies were occupied by the Japanese during the war. At the end of the war, the colony renamed itself Indonesia and declared itself independent. Many people from the former Dutch East Indies moved to the Netherlands. The Dutch did not accept the independence of Indonesia until 1949.

Dutch Guiana became fully independent from the Netherlands as Suriname in 1975. Up to 1981, it was possible for Surinamers to choose between a Surinamese or a Dutch nationality. About 10,000 chose to take the Dutch nationality.

The Netherlands Antilles has self-government but is part of the Kingdom of the Netherlands.

### Postwar Revival

The Netherlands was left in tatters by the war. It had to rebuild its economy and attend to the social needs of the people. America's Marshall Plan injected the finances and the Dutch tackled the problems with their customary vigor. In 1948 the Netherlands formed the Benelux customs union with Belgium and Luxembourg. In the same year Queen Wilhelmina, who had returned after the war, abdicated after nearly sixty years on the throne, and her daughter Juliana succeeded her.

In 1949 the Netherlands became a founding member of NATO. Trade and industry revived, helped by the wealth brought through the discovery of natural gas fields in the North Sea. Unemployment fell so dramatically that there was a shortage of labor and thousands of migrants were welcomed into the country from Italy, Spain, Germany, Greece, Turkey, and Morocco. These people joined immigrants from the former Dutch East Indies, the Antilles, and Suriname to create an increasingly multicultural society.

In 1958, the Netherlands became a founding member of the European Economic Community. The increased prosperity that resulted from economic recovery enabled the government to address many social problems and a number of social programs were introduced. The paternalistic Dutch welfare system was established.

### A Time for Change

The 1960s saw the start of widespread change. Amsterdam became a gathering point for hippies from America, and the protest demonstrations by students and trade unionists that were sweeping through other countries struck a sympathetic chord in the Netherlands. An anarchist group called the Provos was formed, with the express intention of undermining authority. At first they did not enjoy public support. However, attitudes changed in 1965, when police set upon protesters in Spui Square, Amsterdam, in a needlessly brutal manner. The media questioned the way that the authorities were handling the matter, and members of the public raised concerns. Add to this the growing impact of television, and the breakdown of "pillarization," and it is little wonder that a sea change took place. Perhaps because Dutch society had been so rigidly confined, the generation that emerged in the 1960s took the opposite stance and became extremely liberal. At the same time, there was no Dutch secular conservative political party to challenge the dramatic changes; the orthodox Calvinists for their part simply withdrew. Liberal laws on soft drugs, homosexuality, abortion, divorce, prostitution, and euthanasia were swept through on the tide of change.

In the early 1980s unemployment rose and attitudes began to harden against people who were taking unfair advantage of the generous welfare system. Questions also began to be asked about the number of immigrants and asylum seekers entering the country, and the lack of integration of some sections of the immigrant community.

The Netherlands entered the twenty-first century with a buoyant economy. Unemployment had fallen dramatically and businesses were thriving. However, since the tragic events of September 11, 2001, the economy has slowed down. The world economic decline has had an effect on Dutch levels of trade and investment, and unemployment has started to rise. Things are still comfortable, but it will be interesting to see how the Netherlands responds to the challenges that the future holds.

## CITIES IN THE NETHERLANDS

### The Hague

Until 1806, The Hague (*Den Haag*) was the capital of the Netherlands, although it had never been granted city status (rivals Leiden and Delft having blocked the grant of a charter). The *Stadhouder* William II, the Count of Holland, built a castle for himself there in 1250. In 1511, the High Court of Holland was established in The Hague and it became recognized as the administrative and judicial center of the

Netherlands. Later, in 1578, The Hague also became the seat of government when the States-General began to hold its meetings there. When the House of Orange became the royal family in 1814 their official residence remained at The Hague. By this time, however, Amsterdam had become the capital.

When Napoleon sent his brother Louis Bonaparte to govern the Netherlands in 1806, The Hague was little more than a village. Louis decided to establish his court in the more worldly Amsterdam, which he made the capital, although he did grant The Hague city status by way of compensation.

Nowadays, The Hague is the third-largest city in the Netherlands, with a population of 457,726. It is the seat of Dutch government and the official residence of Queen Beatrix. The *Binnenhof* (Inner Court) and *Buitenhof* (Outer Court) are the two chambers of Parliament and the *Ridderzaal* (Knight's Hall, a restored thirteenth-century building) is used for ceremonial occasions, such as the delivery of the Queen's Speech each September.

The International Court of Justice and the Academy of International Law are also in The Hague, as are many of the foreign embassies. It is a refined, elegant, and cultured city, well worth a visit for its museums, art galleries, and upscale shops.

## Amsterdam

The capital of the Netherlands, Amsterdam has a population of 735,526. It is the largest Dutch city and the financial center of the country. It is also one of the key cultural centers and a big draw for tourism. It has a beautiful canal circle (the *grachten gordel*) dating from the start of the seventeenth century. A canal boat trip is the best way to appreciate the magnificent merchant houses that were built alongside the canals. It is famous for its cultural heritage, and there are excellent theaters, concert

halls, museums, and art galleries to be found. Last but not least, Amsterdam is world-famous for its red-light district and for its "coffee shops," where soft drugs are sold for personal use. The city is an exotic blend of people from different backgrounds. It has a lively and fascinating mixture of subcultures, ranging from "hippy" to student (there are two universities), to business—and, of course, the tourists.

## Rotterdam

The second-largest city is Rotterdam, with a population of 598,660. Situated at the mouth of the Maas River, Rotterdam was first established as a port in the thirteenth century when it served the textile towns of Delft and Leiden. It thrived until the seventeenth century when Amsterdam took precedence because it was the seat of the Dutch East India Company. At the start of World War II, the Germans bombed Rotterdam and razed it to the ground, as a warning to the Dutch of what would happen if they did not submit to German occupation. After the war the Dutch government was determined to reestablish the Netherlands as a trading country. Rotterdam was rebuilt as a modern industrial and commercial city, and the largest port in the world. It is now renowned for its architecture and its unique atmosphere—modern and vibrant, with economic and commercial muscle but a cultural heart.

Amsterdam, Rotterdam, The Hague, and Utrecht are the cities that form the *Randstad* ("Rim Town"). As we have seen, most of the population lives in this area, which forms the commercial hub of the country. However, with the improvement of the transport network and of communications technology it has been possible to extend the commercial area further afield and today many other cities and large towns have attracted industry.

Each of the twelve provinces in the Netherlands has its own capital town or city.

## THE DUTCH ROYAL FAMILY

The Dutch generally regard their royal family with affection and respect. They are proud that their royals are more informal than the British and that Queen Beatrix is a hard worker. The premise of "*Doe maar gewoon . . .*" (see Chapter 2) also applies to the royal family. Although they occasionally receive some criticism, and scandals occur, they continue to be held in high regard.

## THE GOVERNMENT

The Netherlands is a constitutional monarchy. There are three levels of government—central, provincial, and local. Central government, based at The Hague, is responsible for overseeing the other two levels. The Queen confirms the Prime Minister and plays an active part in forming the cabinet. The historical name for the Parliament is the States-General (*Staten-Generaal*). This has two chambers—the First Chamber (*Eerste Kamer*) and the Second Chamber (*Tweede Kamer*). The country's twelve provincial councils indirectly elect members for a four-year period to the seventy-five seats in the First Chamber. This has a controlling function. It can ask the Heads of the Ministries and the State Secretaries to explain their policies. It also has the right to carry out investigations.

The Second Chamber has a hundred and fifty seats. Its members, too, are elected for a four-year term. Its main function is legislation—proposing new laws and suggesting amendments to existing laws. If a bill is accepted by a majority of both chambers, the government is obliged to enact it.

Both bodies have representatives from the main political parties. In the Second Chamber, the allocation of seats is determined by the percentage of the total vote that each party receives—a system of proportional representation. Votes are cast for political policies, not for individuals, and representatives are chosen according to their position on the party list, not for their personal qualities. They do not represent a particular area or constituency.

The large number of political parties makes it difficult to form a government. In order to obtain a reasonable number of seats and to increase their influence in the Second Chamber some of the historical political parties have combined. Dutch governments are usually a coalition of two or three parties.

## LIVING APART TOGETHER

You may well come across the term *verzuiling* in relation to Dutch politics. In the 1960s the old system of "pillarization" began to break down.

Although each of the main religions had its own television and radio stations, it was impossible to control what people were choosing to watch in their own homes. People became exposed to other ideas and realized that the differences between them were not insurmountable. Gradually the barriers between different communities were eroded. At the same time the Dutch became more aware of political movements outside the country, which also influenced public opinion.

In the 1970s and '80s, a different type of "living apart together" was created when growing numbers of immigrants began to enter the Netherlands. Separate communities of different races settled in particular areas. Some kept to their traditional way of life and culture as best as they could. Dutch law enabled and even encouraged this voluntary segregation by making it possible for these communities to set up their own schools, in which children could be taught the cultural norms and values of their original, rather than their adopted, country.

The Dutch are generally keen that everybody should have the right to choose their own way of life. However, concerns started to surface in the 1980s and '90s that instead of the immigrants integrating into Dutch society, in some parts of the Netherlands Dutch culture was gradually being displaced by that of the new arrivals.

An attempt was made to address these concerns. In the 1990s laws were introduced to ensure that foreigners coming to settle long-term in the Netherlands learned the Dutch language and culture, in order to be able to contribute to the economy as quickly as possible. However, the issue of immigration did not go away and it resurfaced when it was taken up by a new arrival on the political stage—Pim Fortuyn.

## THE LEGACY OF PIM FORTUYN

The democratic process is at the heart of Dutch politics. It is regarded as vital that voters can choose a party whose policies match their own views. In order for the system of proportional representation to function, it is essential to look for common ground and focus on areas of agreement. The strengths of this system lie in the harmonious working relationship that it creates— getting along together, not being extreme, taking a middle road, and showing a tolerance for all groups within society.

However, there are also disadvantages. First, it encourages the practice of "making do" and glossing over important differences, putting them to one side rather than tackling them head on. Second, it can be slow and laborious. Forming a coalition government after the elections can take months of difficult negotiations. Third, the resulting coalition may not truly reflect the result at the ballot box. Coalitions can be formed by a number of parties with few seats in the Second Chamber, rather than between the parties that obtained the most votes. This can lead to a situation where the status quo is preserved at the cost of not solving underlying problems.

In 2001 Pim Fortuyn brought all this out into the open. He swept on to the political scene in a way that shocked politicians and many members of the public, but which delighted others. He was a flamboyant character—a homosexual who rode around in a chauffeur-driven, pink Daimler. His behavior shook the establishment to the core. It did not particularly matter that he was homosexual, but Dutch politicians are supposed to be low key, not charismatic populists.

Fortuyn certainly stirred things up! He decried the constant discussion and debate strangling Dutch politics. He wanted politicians to tackle major issues in a practical manner, particularly transport and healthcare, and to stop papering over the cracks between parties in the coalition.

He declared that the Dutch were no longer prepared to put up with the official levels of tolerance imposed by law to protect the rights of minorities. The next government would need to acknowledge people's concerns by limiting immigration and restricting the leeway given to minority groups. Most people were appalled. He was likened to Le Pen, and even to Mussolini. The party that had chosen him as its leader—*Leefbaar Nederland* (Livable Netherlands)—dropped him after he made racist remarks in an interview. Undeterred, he went ahead to form his own party—*Lijst Pim Fortuyn* (LPF). He was in the middle of a colorful election campaign when an animal rights activist assassinated him in May 2002.

Fortuyn's murder rocked the nation. No public figure had been killed in the Netherlands since 1584 and the Dutch were shocked. They regarded it as an attack upon democracy itself, and on the right of people to speak their mind. Fortuyn's political party received over a million votes in the general election after his murder. Some commentators saw this extraordinary result as a protest by a section of society against the killing of a public figure, not as support for his views. Others interpreted it as a clear indication that public opinion was starting to turn against the Dutch tradition of tolerance.

The whole situation turned into a shambles when the LPF Party members quarreled so bitterly among themselves that they could not form part of a coalition government. Their supporters were disillusioned and left in droves.

New elections took place and the political party representing traditional values, the CDA, took the most seats, with the center-left party, the PvdA, coming in a close second.

Pim Fortuyn's legacy seems to have been to make the Dutch people reexamine the worth of their current system. The public appears to be growing impatient with the indecisiveness of its politicians. The failure to form a coalition after new elections in January 2003 was viewed by many as bordering on incompetent—especially with war in Iraq looming and an economic downturn in the offing. The next few years may well prove crucial in measuring the Dutch public's desire for more radical change.

## THE DUTCH IN THE EU

The Netherlands was one of the founding members of the European Union. After World War II there was a move toward greater European integration. In May 1948, Princess Juliana and Prince Bernhard hosted the Congress of Europe in The Hague. This was the first step on the road to a European Union. In 1952, six European countries—the Netherlands, Belgium, France, Germany, Italy, and Luxembourg—combined to form the European Coal and Steel Community (ECSC) to bring the industries under common control for economic and security reasons. In 1958 the Dutch Minister of Foreign Affairs played an important role in setting up the European Economic Community (EEC).

The Netherlands has been keen from the start to have an influence on the ideas, policies, and laws to emerge from the Union, especially with regard to commercial and social issues. In 1967 the ECSC, the EEC, and the European Atomic Energy Community joined together to form the European Communities (EC). In 1973, three more countries joined the EC, including Britain, and more have joined since then.

The Maastricht Summit, held in the Netherlands in 1991, was crucial in laying the foundations for economic and monetary union. When the Maastricht Treaty came into force in 1993, the EC became the European Union. As a trading nation, the Netherlands has supported the creation of a single market and the removal of trade barriers. As a small country within Europe it has regarded the EU as a security measure—ensuring that the interests of the larger states do not override the concerns of smaller ones. The EU gives the Netherlands a voice and representation in a body that has a common purpose, and ensures that national interests do not overwhelm the common interest of its members.

The Netherlands is also a member of the Eurozone—the Dutch guilder has been replaced by the euro—which is an indication of the level of its commitment to the EU. However, the Netherlands has not totally embedded itself in Europe. It also keeps an eye on the Atlantic and takes note of what is happening in America and other parts of the world. As a trading nation it needs to keep a finger on the pulse of events in all four corners of the globe.

Generally the Dutch believe strongly in the need for the controlling influence of international law. They recognize the reality of American power, but consider it essential for all NATO members to ensure that they use their power justly and correctly. They are moderate people who value the principles of order, restraint, and justice, and they are not averse to pointing out to other countries, no matter how big and powerful, the error of their ways. Moralistic judgment is often in the background, with the Dutch acting as the self-appointed guardians of the sensible and rational approach.

## THE DUTCH PEOPLE TODAY

Over the centuries, the Dutch spirit has been shaped by the influences of Calvinism and Humanism, and by the Netherlands' role as an international trading nation. Prior to the 1960s

Dutch society was very strict, with rules governing every aspect of behavior. The 1960s and '70s saw a period of radical change. Society swung in the opposite direction, becoming very permissive in reaction to the years of social control. The Dutch revised their respectful view of authority and reconsidered the role of the individual within society. People began to speak up for themselves and to take greater responsibility for their lives. They were far more likely to question decisions made at work, in their local community, and in central government, and to challenge the establishment. With this rise in individualism came the erosion of traditional bonds—religion, politics, social groups, and work associations. Family relationships changed. Individuals were no longer so regulated and "policed" by other family members as they had been up to the 1960s.

In the 1990s the pendulum began to swing back to a more central position. Confidence in the government and in other social institutions was largely restored. The economic boom of the late 1980s and '90s created a feeling of confidence and security. The only perceived threat was the growth of multiculturalism, as large numbers of asylum seekers and economic migrants were admitted to the country. The Dutch responded by calling for immigrants to be required to assimilate themselves into Dutch culture, rather than expecting the host country to incorporate foreign cultures into its way of life.

This situation has resulted in a resolve on the part of some to reaffirm traditional Dutch standards, customs, and values. Other sections of society, of course, have always lived by traditional values and continue to do so. However, the young, and groups that have a lot of contact with other countries, seem to be ready for further change.

This is reflected in the growth of consumerism and ever greater individualism. Some people are ceasing to put social responsibilities before their own needs and desires. The economic situation has recently begun to deteriorate, and economic pressure could lead to even more self-centered behavior. On the other hand, the social conscience of young people who currently reject traditional Dutch values may reawaken. In the next chapter we look in greater depth at what those values are.

# VALUES & ATTITUDES

## THE INFLUENCE OF CALVIN

Much has been made of the fact that Dutch society is built upon Calvinist ethics and values. For the most part today this is a secularized version of Calvinism. People live in modest homes, which they make cozy in order to be pleasantly happy. They do not spend large sums of money, and if they do they keep it quiet. They believe in the value of debate, and the right of individuals to express their opinion before decisions are reached. How do these aspects of Dutch life stem from Calvinist teachings?

John Calvin's strict and uncompromising ideas became increasingly popular in the Netherlands from 1560 onward. His moral code was rigorous. He preached that God determined peoples' fate; therefore, they should know and accept their place in the world and not try to rise above it. All people were equal and material wealth or status meant nothing in religious terms. As men were born with Original Sin, according to Calvin, they should strive to improve themselves and to help others, so that God would forgive them. This formed the religious basis for a social conscience.

These principles were based on the idea that it was necessary to answer to God for your behavior. Calvin believed that the judgment of others was worthwhile if it corresponded with God's purpose and helped individuals both to see the error of their ways and to keep in line with moral requirements. He taught that it was necessary to be sober in lifestyle, to be stoical, and to accept

what life brought. People should put effort into using the talents that God had given them wisely, but not expect congratulations for their achievements, for they would prosper only if it were God's will that they should do so. As a trained lawyer, Calvin presented his ideas in a forceful, rational, and well-argued manner.

Why the Protestant religions were so popular with the Germanic peoples, and with the Dutch in particular, is open to discussion. The Dutch had a choice between Calvinism and Lutheranism, which was a less strict form of Protestantism. The majority of the merchant class chose Calvinism. The very fact that Calvinism was harsh could have been its main appeal: God was seen as a punishing rather than a benevolent and nurturing deity. The vast majority of Dutch people in the sixteenth century lived hard lives, battling for survival against the constant threat of floods and weather, and perhaps they could identify in this the hand of an uncompromising God.

Calvinism probably also appealed to the Dutch because they were a nation of traders and merchants. Calvin proposed that Church and State be separated, and the State given the power to regulate society. The wealthy burghers were attracted by a religion that told people to accept their lot and be content with their position in society. They were at the top of the pecking order, and any doctrine that helped preserve their position in society was bound to be appealing.

Lutheranism may have been rejected because it was more tolerant of many traditional Catholic practices. The merchants regarded it as unfair to be toiling in order to line the pockets of the Church. They also resented the payment of exorbitant taxes to the Catholic King of Spain.

Interestingly, the Calvinist ethos still holds sway today, even though there are currently more Catholics than Protestants in the Netherlands, of whom only a small portion are Calvinists. In the four and a half centuries that have passed since the emergence of Dutch Calvinism many of its values have become embedded in Dutch society as a whole.

Calvinist rigor has been tempered by the teachings of Erasmus, who believed in the intrinsic goodness of humankind and the need for humane and nonviolent behavior in the resolution of disputes. This combination of Calvinist and Humanist values lies at the heart of key institutions in the Netherlands, such as the government, and informs the laws of the land. It would require a revolution in Dutch society to pry it out and replace it with something else. On the whole, the Dutch are proud of their values and in no hurry to change them. They provide stability and continuity in a changing world.

There are certainly aspects of Dutch behavior that can be frustrating and difficult for an outsider to accept or understand, but at its core is respect for others and the desire to live in harmony—enabling everybody to be happy.

## EGALITARIANISM AND DEMOCRACY
The Dutch consider it very important that all citizens have equal rights. In practical terms, this means constant consultation with representatives

from each section of the community. Many local meetings are held to try to take everyone's requirements and opinions into account. This can prove very difficult when the opinions being expressed are extremely diverse.

Active citizenship underpins Dutch society. In the Netherlands, people not only have a *right* to get involved, but they also have a *duty* to do so. As a result, children are taught to express their opinions and to feel that they have a right to be heard. This prepares them to become the sort of adults who will participate well in Dutch society, taking advantage of the opportunities given to express their views and to influence the decisions that affect daily life.

## PRIDE

The Dutch are a proud nation, and justifiably so. As a local saying goes, "God made the Earth, but the Dutch made Holland." They have conquered the sea, in order to make the best use of the area available to them, and their engineers have an excellent reputation throughout the world. Their nation is very small, but it is one of the wealthiest in the world, with a high standard of living. They are also renowned for their ability in trade and the success of their commercial maritime empire.

At times, however, this pride can seem to outsiders to have an arrogant and judgmental tone—the Dutch know best. There is a propensity to give advice when it has not been asked for.

## ADDED VALUE AND THRIFT

The Dutch are nothing if not resourceful, and the recycling of goods (as well as of paper, glass, compost, etc.) is an integral part of Dutch life. Until recently, any unwanted large items could be left out on the sidewalk for vans to collect. One would often see people sorting through the rubbish—it was perfectly acceptable to take something, after having checked with the original owner. Sidewalk collections are not so common now, but the same process takes place in the local *kringloopcentrum* (recycling center), where all the larger items are gathered to sell to new owners.

## MODESTY

Talking about personal finances is generally unacceptable, and ostentatious behavior is discouraged, certainly by the older generation. Most Dutch people do not aspire to live luxuriously, and their idea of the quality of life is not materialistic. For the Dutch it is not necessary constantly to strive to improve your lot or to prove your success to other people. They believe that you should work to live and not live to work. People in the Netherlands have to justify themselves if they appear to have more than they actually need. For example, the purchase of a large expensive car will be met with inquiries about why it is necessary to have one so big or so powerful. The dominant way of living in the Netherlands is *samenleving* (living together), and that means individuals fitting in with and caring about society as a whole.

The younger generation, however, appears to be changing and conspicuous consumption is becoming more common. This is still frowned upon by older people: if you make too much of your new car or exotic holiday you will be "showing off," and will receive a cool response.

## "DOE MAAR GEWOON..."

*"Doe maar gewoon, want gewoon is gek genoeg!"* means "Behave normally, that's strange enough!" Underlying this expression is the Dutch spirit of egalitarianism and conformity—nobody is better than anybody else and should not think that they are. It is not acceptable to try to get yourself noticed, because setting yourself apart from other people implies that you are superior in some way. In this respect, the Dutch are rather more conformist than the Americans or British.

The point is to fit in with and blend into society. At first, this appears to be at odds with the renowned Dutch tolerance of diversity. These two apparently opposing principles can operate in harmony, however, because, while all manner of views and behavior are tolerated, it is expected that individuals will stick to their own group and not impose their ideas on others. Most people abide by traditional norms of behavior. Those outside are free to choose their way of life, as long as it doesn't encroach upon society. "Living apart together" has enabled the Dutch to tolerate each other from a distance. Multiculturalism has brought new expectations, however, and the norms are being challenged.

Although Dutch laws are liberal, it would be a mistake to think that the broadmindedness of the cities extends to the provinces. Generally, the more rural the area, the more conservative the people. Some areas still have a high percentage of strictly religious people, and liberal views are frowned upon in such communities.

## STOICISM

Among the Dutch it is not generally acceptable to show your emotions in public. This is regarded with a degree of skepticism or embarrassment. The older generation, in particular, was shaped by the hardship of the German occupation in World War II, and has no time for anybody who complains about minor problems or difficulties. The younger generations have been raised to dust themselves off and get on with things. Don't moan! Emotions such as depression or grief are regarded as private matters and are expressed only within the immediate family, if at all. Similarly, try to contain expressions of enjoyment. Effusiveness is regarded with distrust—as an indication of insincerity and superficiality, rather than as a genuine expression of pleasure.

### CLEANLINESS AND HEALTH

Dutch houses are spotlessly clean, inside as well as out. Cleanliness is an ingrained value that holds good for most Dutch people. Its origins lie in the Calvinist belief that cleanliness is next to godliness, and the idea that people who are gainfully employed in housework are not wasting time on idle chatter or other mischief.

Nowadays, religious belief is not so widespread, but keeping one's home clean and tidy is still regarded as important. It is a way of providing the family with a healthy environment, as well as avoiding the censure of others. If a Dutch woman notices that your windows are dirty, she is likely to point it out.

## DUTCH HONESTY

Many people are struck by the forthright nature of the Dutch. As we have seen, they are positively encouraged from childhood to voice their opinions. This spills over into personal exchanges, and can be hard to handle if taken as criticism, rather than as a comment. They also prefer you to tell them what you really think, and are wary of what they regard as excessive politeness. They do not generally say "please" and "thank you" as often as English-speakers do.

### Be Yourself

A British woman visiting a Dutch friend was offered a cup of coffee. "*Ja graag*" ("Yes please"), she replied. Upon being offered milk and sugar she answered in the same manner, and again, when offered a cookie she said "Thank you" ("*Dank je wel*"). Irritated, her Dutch friend told her she didn't have to say please and thank you *all* the time. The visitor felt rather hurt, and replied that her manners were part of her upbringing, and not something she was willing to abandon in order to fit in. The Dutch woman accepted this explanation with a smile, and her "excessive" politeness was never remarked upon again.

The Dutch can be suspicious of overfamiliarity from people who do not know them well. The right to be regarded as a friend has to be earned. Once this has been achieved, your Dutch friends will be extremely loyal to you and will help you out in any way that they can when you are in need.

## GEZELLIGHEID

The feeling of *gezelligheid* is central to Dutch social life. The dictionary defines *gezellig* as "cozy," but "congenial" is possibly more accurate, describing a situation or atmosphere that is relaxed and full of fellow feeling. *Gezelligheid* is about people enjoying themselves in the company of others—it is not about being at home alone. If a Dutch person tells you that time spent with you was *gezellig*, you can take it that they enjoyed themselves and felt relaxed and at ease in your company—a compliment!

## COMMUNITY SPIRIT

*Gezelligheid* is also related to living harmoniously with others—being considerate in order to get along well. Conformity to social rules is seen as the basis of security, and community spirit is an essential part of Dutch life. This manifests itself in the concern shown for vulnerable people in the community and the support available for them.

However, the downside of community spirit and its associated support network is that neighbors are free to comment if they consider that a local resident or group is letting their neighborhood down in any way. This could be about something as trivial as not keeping the garden tidy, or about more extreme behavior, such as creating a major disturbance with too much noise. In America or Britain this sort of intervention would probably be regarded as interference, but in the Netherlands it is an acceptable way of showing concern and maintaining social harmony. In earlier, more religious times, this kind of outspoken criticism was a way of maintaining the respectability of individuals, and by extension the community. Nowadays it is simply a way of keeping people in line with the expectations of their neighbors. It is all part of good citizenship.

People who prefer their own company and are not sociable may be accused of being *ongezellig*. If they decline to join in with communal activities—the idea being to have fun and enjoy things as part of a group, rather than as an individual—they are regarded as not playing a proper part in society. If you are not a naturally gregarious person, be prepared to put yourself out and participate in group activities if you want to be accepted by your Dutch acquaintances and friends.

Many Dutch people—especially women and
the newly retired—demonstrate their community
spirit by working voluntarily for locally based
organizations. Their contribution is valued and
encouraged. Volunteers are organized through a
central agency in each main town and prizes are
awarded every year to people who have made
exceptional contributions.

## RELIGION

After the loss of the Catholic southern provinces,
Calvinism predominated in the Netherlands.
Although tolerated, other religions were not given
equal rights until the late eighteenth century.

In the late nineteenth century there was a split
within the Dutch Reformed Church (*Nederlands
Hervormde Kerk*). The theologian and politician
Abraham Kuyper (1837–1920) established the
more strictly Calvinistic *Gereformeerde Kerk* (or
Reformed Church). Kuypers considered that the
national Dutch Reformed Church was far too
liberal. He stood for a return to the strict
teachings of the Reformation period. He
promoted the idea that members of the new
Reformed Church should isolate themselves from
other communities, so that they would not be
"besmirched" or influenced by other beliefs. This
was the start of "pillarization" in Dutch society.

Pillarization came to an end when religious belief began to decline and people realized that they could share political goals even if their religions were different. Thus the CDA (Christian Democrat Appeal) is a fusion of a Catholic and two Calvinist political parties. Fewer people attend church nowadays, or belong to a particular religious community. Nevertheless, 60 percent of the population identifies with a religious faith.

There are, however, still certain parts of the country where the *Gereformeerde Kerk* is influential—in the so-called "Bible Belt," which takes in a number of towns and villages in a diagonal line across the country from Zeeland up to the northwest of the Overijssel Province. Within the Bible-Belt some people still dress in traditional costume and members of the Reformed Church embrace orthodox Calvinistic doctrine. There, for example, it is not acceptable for people to work—to clean cars or mow lawns—on a Sunday, which is reserved for religious devotion. The Calvinists have an extensive knowledge of the Bible and are expected to adhere to its teachings literally.

Members of the mainstream Protestant *Hervormde Kerk* have far more liberal views than members of the *Gereformeerde Kerk*. Catholics in the Netherlands tend to be less rigid on the whole than strict Roman Catholics elsewhere.

# CUSTOMS & TRADITIONS

The Dutch celebrate a wide variety of national events. Some have religious origins, others historical significance. For the most part, they provide a great reason for having a party. The importance of communal life is reflected in their pride in the larger community—the nation as a whole—and in their smaller communities—towns, villages, and neighborhoods. This pride is demonstrated and shared through communal celebrations and having a *gezellig* time together.

## NATIONAL FESTIVALS
National festivals provide an opportunity for visitors to mingle with the locals and share in the enjoyment. The following are the main events in the order that they occur during the year.

### January 1—New Year's Day (*Nieuwjaarsdag*)
You can normally still hear fireworks going off on New Year's Day but nowhere near to the extent that they do on New Year's Eve! Many people spend the day quietly after the celebrations the night before. It is often a time for people to get

some fresh air and exercise by going out for a walk, cycling, or ice-skating if the weather is very cold.

### February—Carnival (*Carnaval*)

This takes place on the weekend before Fat (Shrove) Tuesday and is celebrated by the Catholic communities. Everybody (children included) dresses up in wonderful bright costumes and takes part in parades. There is usually a huge party.

### April 1—April Fool's Day

Practical jokes are elevated to an art form. People play them on each other, and almost all the newspapers and Dutch television channels take part in the fun by covering a "story" that turns out later to be a hoax.

### *Media Fun*

VPRO Radio (the Liberal Protestant Radio network) once "covered" a strange affliction that had struck Rembrandt's painting *The Night Watch*. The paint had begun to peel off slowly but surely, and the whole image was expected to vanish by midnight. The National Gallery would reopen at 8:00 p.m. so that art-lovers countrywide could cast one last glance at the famous painting. A considerable crowd gathered in front of the museum. It was not until reporters from VPRO Radio began to interview them that people caught on that it was a gigantic April Fool's joke.

## April—National Museum Weekend (*Nationaal Museumweekend*)

This event is normally held on the third weekend in April. Free entry to all the museums gives everybody the chance to have a cultural day out. Naturally, many people take advantage of this and the museums are usually packed.

## April 30—Queen's Day (*Koninginnedag*)

This is a major holiday. When Queen Beatrix ascended the throne, the Dutch decided to leave the official celebration on her mother's birthday. In doing so, they continued to honor Queen Juliana and avoided moving the holiday to January, which is too cold for the outdoor activities that accompany the occasion.

Red, white, and blue national flags, and orange ensigns for the House of Orange, festoon the houses. Each year, as part of the festivities, the Queen and her family pay an official visit to two towns, where they are received with great acclaim. On *Koninginnedag* many towns hold fairs, and the streets are full of families selling their secondhand goods, displayed on the ground on blankets, or on stands in the market squares. Children are out in force, too—selling their old toys or clothes, and playing musical instruments to earn a bit of money from passers-by. Everybody is dressed in orange clothes or wigs and great fun is had by all. A lot of rubbish is on sale, but there are also some good bargains to be found.

## May—First Herring Catch Auction

The first herring catch of the season is celebrated with a ceremony at the end of May. The Queen is offered the *Koninneharing*—the best herring of the catch. The first barrel of herrings is auctioned off, with the proceeds going to charity.

## National Windmill Day (*Nationale Molendag*)

This holiday is normally held on the second Saturday in May. Many of the country's working windmills are open to the public.

## November 11—St. Martin's Day (*Sint Maarten's Dag*)

Small groups of children carrying paper lanterns go from door to door in their local neighborhood to sing and collect sweets and other treats from their neighbors. If you try to give them more than one sweet, they look embarrassed, and tell you quite seriously that it isn't necessary. They are obviously well-briefed about what to expect and what it is reasonable to accept.

## Mid November to early December—St. Nicholas (*Sinterklaas*)

The historical St. Nicholas (*Sinterklaas*) was Bishop of Myra in Lycia, in present-day Turkey, in the fourth century CE. The ancient celebration of his feast day was made optional by the Roman Catholic Church in 1968, although it was stressed that there was no doubt about his authenticity. St. Nicholas is known as the friend and protector of people in need. He is the patron saint of children, sailors, scholars, travelers, and merchants, to name but a few.

"*Sinterklaas*" arrives in Amsterdam on a boat from Spain with his Moorish servants—the Black Peters (*Zwarte Pieten*). He tours the country on a white horse, visiting all the main towns to the great excitement of the children. Some are in awe of him, because their parents tell them that he knows all about them—who has been good during the year and who has been bad.

The *Zwarte Pieten* throw cookies and sweets to the children and generally clown around, singing, or playing musical instruments. Children used to be told that they would take naughty children away in their sacks and only give sweets to the good ones. This aspect is now played down, so as not to perpetuate racist stereotypes. The *Zwarte Pieten* are still mainly white people with their faces blackened to look like Moors, and this is generally accepted. For American and British visitors it can be a bit of a shock!

*Sinterklaas's* birthday is celebrated by families, especially those with younger children, on December 5 with *pakjesavond* (present evening). On the days leading up to *pakjesavond* the children put out an empty shoe at night, and

*Sinterklaas* leaves them a few chocolates or sweets. On *pakjesavond* itself, people give each other *surprises*, presents that are normally fairly inexpensive but are chosen with great care and cleverly wrapped to disguise the contents. They are given with a poem, supposedly penned by *Sinterklaas* and the *Zwarte Pieten*, that is a humorous portrait of the recipient's good points and weaknesses. These poems can be pretty sharp. They also often refer to activities that the recipient enjoys, and the "surprise" may be related to this activity—for example a mock-computer or a football. On December 6, *Sinterklaas* returns to Spain until the next year.

### December 24 and 25—Christmas Day and Boxing Day (*Eerste Kerstdag* and *Tweede Kerstdag*)

These have traditionally been low-key occasions in comparison with *Sinterklaas*, with people attending church, having a Christmas tree, and exchanging cards and a few presents. They would celebrate in a quiet manner within the family. The festival has, however, become far more commercial recently, and is threatening to obscure *Sinterklaas*.

### December 31—New Year's Eve (*Oud en Nieuw*)

The New Year is celebrated by setting off thousands of fireworks at midnight. There are few organized firework displays, other than in the larger cities. Fireworks can be ordered and collected from licensed businesses in the days running up to New Year's Eve, but it is illegal to set them off before the holiday itself. Not that this stops crowds of boys gathering on street corners and setting off chains of firecrackers!

Individuals at family gatherings light most of the fireworks between midnight and 1:00 a.m. on New Year's Eve/Day. Safety does not seem to be given very high priority, and there are accidents each year, despite warnings on television. If you are at all worried it is best to stay and watch from indoors, although you will miss some of the atmosphere of the event. People gather on the street just after midnight (having first drunk a toast to their family members inside their houses) to shake hands and wish each other well for the year to come. It is a friendly atmosphere. Typical treats are *appelflappen*—fried battered apple rings—and *olliebollen*—a kind of doughnut filled with raisins.

## ANNUAL SPECIAL EVENTS

A number of special events are held throughout the country on an annual basis. They include:

**March:** The European Fine Art Fair, Maastricht— a huge fine arts and antiques fair in south

Limburg that attracts international dealers from around the world.

**April:** Flower Parade *Bollenstreek*—taking place between Haarlem and Noordwijk in the last week of April, with colorful floats and a parade.

**May/June:** Jazz and blues music festivals are held in many towns nationwide.

**June:** *Pinkpop*, an open-air pop festival, which is part of Gay Pride week.

**June/July:** The Holland Festival—a cultural event held in Amsterdam with ballet, theater, opera, music, and film. Also the open-air Vondelpark Festival, with free performances of dance, children's theater, plays, and music in the park.

**July:** North Sea Jazz Festival, held in The Hague. A big event, with internationally renowned jazz bands in open-air performances throughout the city.

**August:** *Uitmarkt*—free music and theater performances in Amsterdam to mark the end of one theater season and the start of the next.

**September:** Flower Parade, taking place between Aalsmeer, where many of the Netherland's key

flower auction houses are based, and Amsterdam,
in early September, with colorful floats, bands, and
drum majorettes. Also in September, the Jordaan
Festival is held in one of the oldest parts of
Amsterdam. It is a large street party to celebrate
life in the area. Monument Day (*Monumentendag*)
is held on the second Saturday of the month. This
is the chance to see inside historical buildings that
are usually closed to the public.

There are many more special activities on offer
nationwide. For details, see the *Er-op-Uit* guide,
published every March, available at railway stations. It
contains a calendar (*uitkalendar*) with a huge variety
of events for the coming year in all the main towns.

## FAMILY CELEBRATIONS

As we have seen, the family is important to the
Dutch, and family celebrations are a time for
everybody to get together (with their friends too)
to relax and have some fun.

### Birthdays

These are important occasions. The family and
friends get together at the home of the person
whose birthday it is, and everyone brings a small
present. It is not necessary to give something
expensive, but find out what the person would
like by asking a close family member. A *verlanglijst*
(wish list) may have been compiled by the
birthday person. The Dutch send birthday

cards only if they cannot attend the celebration.

Do learn to say "*Gefeliciteerd!*" If you are invited to a birthday party, you will hear people congratulating the birthday person, "*Gefeliciteerd met je verjaardag!*" They will also congratulate everybody else present, particularly the relatives of the person whose birthday it is, but also most of the guests. "*Gefeliciteerd met de verjaardag van je zoon!*" or "*je vrouw*" or "*je moeder.*" ("Congratulations on your son's birthday . . . your wife's birthday . . . your mother's birthday.")

Birthday parties are normally an open-house event, without formal invitations. If you have been before, you are expected to come again, and if you cannot do so, you had better have a very good reason. You may be asked to come at a particular time—ask, if you are not sure, when would be most convenient for your host(ess). Generally speaking, guests just arrive throughout the day, from about 10:00 a.m. onward. You will be served coffee and cake or sweet pastry. After two cups of coffee, you will be offered an alcoholic or soft drink, and savory snacks will be handed around. Do not stay all day, no matter how *gezellig* it is.

A fiftieth birthday is a special occasion. The birthday person is traditionally said to have reached an age of maturity and wisdom, and they are known as a "Sarah" (lady) or an "Abraham" (man). You may see a large straw doll of a man or a woman in the front garden of a house with banners and flags

proclaiming "*Gefeliciteerd Wout/ Hennie/*whoever—
*50 vandaag!*"—"Congratulations Wout
/Hennie/whoever—50 today!" One-hundredth
birthdays are also marked with great ceremony.

## Weddings

These are also celebrated with gusto. In the
Netherlands all weddings take place in
the *gemeentehuis* (town hall) with
a civic ceremony in order to be
legally recognized. The couple can
also choose to have a church
service. There is often a celebration meal for
members of the close family, and then a larger
party or reception for other relatives, friends, and
acquaintances. If you want to buy a gift for the
happy couple, the invitation will include the name
and telephone number (or e-mail address) for the
*Ceremoniemeester* (Master of Ceremonies), who
will have a gift list. If money is requested put the
check or cash into an envelope with a card and
post it into the box provided at the reception.

At a larger party, it is usual for close relatives
to have composed a song (normally with far too
many verses) relating something funny about the
couple and generally teasing them. There may be
a homemade video in a similar vein.

## Birth of a Baby

The birth of a baby is announced to the whole
neighborhood. The front garden of the proud

parents' home is decked out with pink or blue flags, balloons, a "washing line" with pink or blue doll's clothes, and a large cardboard stork with the baby's date of birth, name, and weight written on it. The parents will usually also send out announcement cards inviting family and friends to visit the new addition to the family within set times during the day, or by appointment. You should take a small gift for the baby—clothing, a photo album, or toy—and flowers for the mother. You will be given a cup of coffee or tea (which the Dutch drink weak with sugar, if required, but not with milk) and a *beschuit met muisjes*—a sort of rusk with tiny aniseed sweets in pink or blue on the top.

## Wedding Anniversaries

Not everyone celebrates wedding anniversaries, but some are considered special and may prompt a party—the twelve-and-a-half-years', twenty-fifth, and fiftieth particularly. Sometimes you will be asked by a family member to contribute to a special book that is being compiled for the couple, with stories, for example, from their actual wedding day. There is often also a *Ceremoniemeester* to dispense advice. You will probably be asked to join in singing a song for the couple that has been specially composed by friends or family. A sheet of words is provided—if you can't read or understand them, just hum the chorus!

## Retirement Parties

These are normally provided by the organization from which the person is retiring. The "retiree" is allowed to invite a number of people from work and home for coffee and cake or a buffet—how elaborate depends on the organization. A collection is made at work for a gift (see also Chapter 8) and people coming from outside the company bring their own present. It is more important to choose something that reflects the interests of the recipient than to buy an expensive present.

## HISTORICAL OCCASIONS

Some of the national events in the year have an historical origin or context. The main ones are listed below.

**May 4:** Remembrance Day (*Dodenherdenking*). The official commemoration day for all the people killed in World War II. Flags are hung at half-mast outside people's houses and memorial services are held. At 8:00 p.m. there is a two-minute silence, which the vast majority of the population respects, in remembrance of the dead.

**May 5:** Liberation Day (*Bevrijdingsdag*). This celebrates the liberation of the Netherlands by the Allied Forces in 1945. Flags are hung outside people's houses.

**June–August:** Local festivals and fairs are held in many towns nationwide. These are often celebrations of historical events or of specific folk traditions. They give a special insight into the history and customs of the different parts of the Netherlands.

**September:** State Opening of Parliament (*Prinsjesdag*). Held in The Hague on the third Tuesday in September. The Queen rides in a golden horse-drawn coach from her palace to Parliament, accompanied by members of her family. The streets are lined with cheering people.

# chapter four

# MAKING FRIENDS

The Dutch are very sociable—with family, long-standing friends, and in the local community. Living closely together is very much part of Dutch life (literally, in urban areas), and they spend time building up relationships in order to maintain harmony in the *samenleving* (society). As a result, they are generally at ease in social situations, good at making conversation, and relaxed in their manner. They are usually interested in other people and keen to make visitors feel welcome and comfortable, but there are a couple of exceptions to this. In the cities, people may be too busy to spare much time for making new friends. Also, people in very rural areas may be more reluctant to make contact with strangers, although once the initial barriers have been overcome the Dutch instinct for hospitality will normally assert itself.

The Dutch are taught the value of social interaction from an early age, when they are expected to make an effort to attend social events and join in. This carries on into adult life, and a Dutch family ends up with rather a lot of commitments—family events, regular contact with friends, activities at clubs or societies, and often involvement with the local community. Certain conventions keep this busy social life under control and running smoothly. The Dutch tend to make appointments, rather than to visit spontaneously, and it is generally understood how long certain types of visit will last.

## ATTITUDES TO FOREIGNERS

The Dutch are generally friendly toward foreigners and will help out if you ask for assistance. If you want to talk to somebody, it is appreciated if you try to speak a bit of Dutch, although your attempts may well be met with a slightly wry smile. "*Spreekt u Engels alstublieft?*" is the polite way to ask if someone speaks English. Normally, at the sound of an American or British accent, the person will switch immediately to English to reply. The Dutch are good at languages—great importance is placed on learning languages in schools—and they are normally delighted to speak to you in English.

The majority of the population does not tolerate racist attitudes, and people are generally pleasant. The recent war in Iraq has altered the attitude of some toward America and Britain. You may have a slightly cool reception, but politeness and hospitality are so ingrained in Dutch behavior that you are unlikely to notice.

If you are staying in the country for a while, you may find that people invite you home. Enjoy the occasion, but do not be too upset if you are not invited again. Many Dutch people are curious about people from abroad and take the opportunity to find out more about them by being sociable. However, they are sometimes too tied up with family and old friends to have much time over to invest in new ones. If you feel you have "clicked" with somebody and want to take the friendship further, take the initiative and persevere, but if a suggestion to get together is declined more than twice, you would be wise to back off or you will be regarded as troublesome.

There is a saying in the Netherlands: "*De kat uit de boom kijken.*" This translates as "The cat looks on from the safety of the tree," or, "Being curious but wary!" This is a good description of a small section of Dutch society. These are older people, often in rural communities, who are interested in foreigners but a bit unsure about getting involved with them, possibly because they are not confident about speaking other languages. If you want to meet them, it will be up to you to learn some basic Dutch and to make the first move. Inviting people home to experience an occasion that is typical of your culture is one way to break the ice, although if it is too different it may be rather intimidating. A normal coffee morning, Dutch style, is a safe start. Have some "props" on hand—a few photos or pictures of your hometown or country perhaps—to help the conversation along, and keep it fairly short until the relationship gets on a more relaxed footing.

## HOW TO MEET THE DUTCH

It is easy to meet people if you are prepared to be proactive and do not wait for others to come to you. The Dutch do not make a strict distinction between work and social life, and it is possible to make friends with colleagues and meet on a social basis. Also, many Dutch people join a sports club or activity group. This is an ideal way to meet people with similar interests. It is also easier to communicate with people who are not very confident in their spoken English if you are doing something practical.

The important thing about making contact with Dutch people is to be prepared to put some effort into it and to persevere in the face of rejection. The onus is on you to convince them of the value of your friendship. This can take a while, but once it has been achieved you will have made loyal friends who will stick with you. In the meantime, enjoy the opportunity to meet all kinds of different people until you find those individuals you would like to know better. If you move into a house or apartment, introduce yourself to the neighbors and invite them over for coffee.

Also, be direct. Do not say "yes" to a Dutch person if you only mean "maybe," and don't say "maybe" if you already know that the answer is "no!" They will just find your prevarication irritating and rude. If you say that you would like to meet up with somebody in the future, you have to mean it when you say it, and, most importantly, follow it up. Otherwise, you will be seen as shallow, and will be given the cold shoulder at your next meeting. Explanations are regarded as poor excuses (*smoesjes*), whether they are or not. In the Dutch view, if it hasn't been worth overcoming the problems to meet your commitments, it would have been better not to make them in the first place.

## VRIENDEN OF KENNISSEN? (FRIENDS OR ACQUAINTANCES?)

Do not assume friendship with Dutch people too quickly. However well you seem to be getting on, they may regard you only as an acquaintance. Don't take this personally. In the same way that the Dutch have two levels of family, they have two levels of friendship. The close family is known as *het gezin*—mother, father, brothers, sisters, and perhaps grandparents. Then there is *de familie*—members of the extended family (aunts, uncles, cousins, etc.). The two levels of friendship are *vrienden*—people they have known for a long time, who have supported their Dutch friend (and have been supported in return) through sad as well as happy times—and *kennissen*—people whom they may regard with affection, but see only occasionally and do not know intimately. *Vrienden* are considered as *trouw*—loyal and reliable. It takes time and effort to be accepted into the close circle of a Dutch person or family and referred to as a *vriend*. If you are referred to as a *kennis* this does not mean that you are disliked or not accepted; it just means that you haven't quite earned your dues yet.

## GREETINGS

Greetings in the Netherlands are fairly formal. When introducing yourself, in either a social or a business situation, you should shake hands, smile, look the other person straight in the eye, and tell them your full name, as in "Good morning. Thomas Parkinson." If they use their first name in *their* greeting, it usually indicates that you can use it when addressing them, but when speaking to people older than yourself use their surname, until they invite you to use their first name. When you leave a social event, you are also expected to shake hands before you go. If there are a lot of people present, you can get away with a general good-bye and wave to the group as a whole, but make sure you shake hands with your hosts. If you are friendly with them, you can give them three light kisses on alternate cheeks, continental style. Men, however, do not generally kiss each other—a firm handshake is fine!

You will find that children are also expected to "give their hand." When arriving at a social event, even very young children are encouraged to go around the group of guests shaking hands and saying a formal "hello." When they leave, they are expected to offer their hand to the hostess to say "thank you" and "good-bye."

## JOINING CLUBS, SOCIETIES, AND CLASSES
Clubs and societies are very popular in the Netherlands, and they exist for all sorts of activities. Joining one is an excellent way of meeting Dutch people who share your interests. To find out what is available, go to the local library, or ask at the *stadhuis* (town hall). The larger cities also have various expatriate clubs,

which may provide some good ways of meeting people—check with your embassy, or have a look at the listings given in the following publications:

*Roundabout*
An English-language "What's on" magazine, available at most railway station newsdealers.

**ACCESS Newsletter**
ACCESS is a nonprofit organization with offices in The Hague and Amsterdam. It provides information to English-speaking people living in the Netherlands on a range of topics, including club/society contact information.

**www.expatica.com**
A Web site with excellent information on all aspects of living in the Netherlands, including club/society listings.

Another good way to make friends is to go to Dutch language classes. Learning even a few phrases will help to smooth the way, and Dutch friends and acquaintances will appreciate the fact that you are trying to fit in. The local *Volksuniversiteiten* offer adult education classes. The further education colleges also run courses;

these are more expensive but are run to standards set by the government.

### GASTVRIJHEID (HOSPITALITY)

The Dutch go to great lengths to make visitors feel welcome. If you are on their territory—be it in a store, office, or house—as a guest, they see it as their responsibility to make the situation as *gezellig* as possible. If you visit an office on a regular basis you are likely to be treated as a colleague after your first couple of visits.

### Invitations Home

If you are invited to a Dutch person's home you should accept if at all possible, because an effort has been made to fit you in to what is usually a busy engagement calendar. If you turn down an invitation it may not be repeated, unless your reason was particularly convincing.

Don't arrive early—this is considered impolite. Arriving more than ten minutes or so late is also frowned upon. And don't expect to be given a tour of the house, as happens in some other countries; this is not a normal part of a visit. You will find that everything is ready for your arrival, and that care has been taken to create a pleasant and welcoming atmosphere.

Never "drop in" for a visit unannounced. The less you know a person, the more notice you need to give. Generally speaking, it is appropriate to give at least a couple of days' notice. Even children call parents, and vice versa, to see if they can come and visit. If you have a *very* good relationship with somebody, you could call in the morning to see if it would be acceptable to pop in later in the day.

## ENTERTAINING

There are certain conventions for entertaining that you should know about. For people at home during the day, morning coffee is an opportunity to catch up with friends or neighbors' news and views. You may be invited to join Dutch friends for morning coffee on the weekend. Strong, freshly brewed coffee will be served (instant coffee is regarded with horror). "*Koffiemelk*" (a sweet condensed milk) or warm frothy milk will be on offer, and there will be cookies or a piece of cake.

Do not take anything until it has been offered to you, as this will be considered bad manners. Even if you have been casually invited to help yourself, take only one biscuit or slice of cake until you are offered again—you are not expected to pig out!

If you are invited to dinner, it will probably start fairly early—generally 6:30 or 7:00 p.m.—and you will be expected to be on time. If a toast is proposed during the meal, the correct word to use is "*proost*" when raising your glass to the people present. After the meal, there will be some more conversation, but do not outstay your welcome—you are unlikely to be allowed to help with the tidying and washing up and your hosts will not want to get to bed too late. During the week, aim to leave between 10:30 and 11:00 p.m. On weekends you could stay longer.

If you are invited to come for a *borrel* (drink), at around 7:30 or 8:00 p.m., this will not be a proper meal. You will need to eat your evening meal before you go, but leave room for *borrelhapjes* (savory snacks). Upon arrival, you may well be offered coffee and a piece of sweet tart to start, followed by a choice of alcoholic or soft drinks, normally with some *borrelhapjes*. Sticking to tea or coffee is considered rather a nuisance and *ongezellig,* so ask for a fruit juice or soft drink if you do not want alcohol.

**GIFT GIVING**

In the Netherlands it is normal to give gifts to people at work on their birthday or on a special occasion, such as a long-service celebration or retirement. Usually, these are given jointly by the team or department and a collection will be made to pay for them. It is not necessary to give a personal or individual present in these situations. Gifts may be given on behalf of the company to visitors from other countries. These are typically corporate gifts with the company logo.

Gift giving is also a part of social life. If you are invited home by Dutch friends and it is the first time that you have been to their house, or if you are going for a meal, it is usual to bring flowers or some special chocolates. Only bring wine if it is good quality. If you are going for morning coffee it is not necessary to bring a gift (unless you are visiting for the first time), although some homemade cookies, typical of your country, will be appreciated. The Dutch do not want you to spend vast amounts on presents. They find this embarrassing and a waste of money, and do not want to feel obliged to do the same in return if they visit you.

# chapter five

# THE DUTCH AT HOME

The Dutch are very family-orientated. At home they combine hard work—keeping it in good condition both outside and within—with a determination to make the most of any opportunities for relaxation and enjoyment.

## QUALITY OF LIFE

The Netherlands is prosperous, and most Dutch people enjoy a good quality of life, although there are poor families, particularly in the bigger cities. Life for the majority is divided between work (paid or voluntary), time in the home or spent with company elsewhere, and enjoyment of the great outdoors. The economic boom of recent years has meant that ordinary people have become increasingly financially secure, and able to spend more on goods and entertainment. The Dutch economy seems to be leveling off now and it remains to be seen what effect this will have on the generally high standard of living.

## LIVING CONDITIONS

Many people live in apartments, although the number of people buying their own houses has increased in recent years.

Apartments and houses are small compared to those in America and Britain, and can seem rather cramped. However, the Dutch have a talent for making the best use of any space available to them. Staircases are narrow and steep so that they occupy as little space as possible. In most houses the attic (the *zolder*) is used as living space and typically comprises a bedroom or two and an area for dealing with laundry.

If you are living in an apartment complex, you will normally find that there are rules about the use of public areas. Before you sign a lease, be certain that you know what your obligations will be as a tenant. If you infringe the rules you will cause offense, and somebody will come to tell you that your behavior is out of order. For example, it is not usually acceptable to leave your belongings in communal areas, such as halls. If you have a balcony, there may be restrictions on what you can put on it. You may also find that you are expected to take part in the maintenance of the communal areas—this is not always carried out by the caretaker or landlord.

Foreigners are often unprepared for this degree of regulation and regard it as intrusive.

### *SCHOON, NETJES, EN GEZELLIG* (CLEAN, NEAT, AND COZY)

The degree to which Dutch houses are kept clean is no mean feat when you consider that many families have two or three children and probably pets as well. Neatness is important because space is at a premium and cannot be wasted under a layer of clutter. It mainly falls to women to ensure that standards are maintained, although children are also taught to help. Perhaps surprisingly, the emphasis on cleanliness and neatness does not result in a cold and unwelcoming atmosphere. Dutch women are very skilled at creating a *gezellig* atmosphere in the home with plants, fresh-flower arrangements, and strategically placed subdued lighting.

### FURNISHINGS

If you are staying for a while and decide to rent, it is advisable to get assistance from an estate agent (*makelaar*). The laws involved and the manner of concluding a contract are so different from

America and Britain that it is worth hiring a professional to act on your behalf. The best way to choose an agent is to ask expatriate acquaintances to recommend someone who has provided a good service for a decent price. Reputable estate agents are members of the Netherlands Estate Agents Foundation (*Nederlandse Vereniging van Makelaars*, or NVM).

There are a few things that you need to be aware of. First of all the description of an apartment or house as "unfurnished" means precisely that. There will be nothing in the apartment at all: no light fittings, floor coverings, or appliances. A semi-furnished property means that there may be floor coverings and some basic appliances, but make sure that you know precisely what is included. A furnished property will usually have nearly everything that you need to move in and function normally—china, cutlery, kitchen appliances, lights, etc. However, do not take for granted items such as a dishwasher, television, video, radio, bedding, or even an oven.

The Dutch do not have room in their apartments and houses for huge refrigerators and freezers, so appliances tend to be small, especially in comparison to those in American homes. Washing machines are small, and they are connected to the cold water supply only. Many visitors buy new appliances in the Netherlands and sell them to other expatriates when they leave.

When you agree to rent a property, you will usually be required to pay the first month's rent in advance, plus a deposit of an extra month or two. Make sure that you know which utilities are included in the rent as this can vary. For those that are your responsibility, arrange for the bills to be sent directly to you so that you can deal with them quickly and efficiently. Be clear about any shared costs, such as a contribution to the upkeep of communal areas. Make a detailed inventory before you move in, listing everything in the property and identifying any problems; otherwise you may end up being charged for repairs to something that was broken before your arrival.

Dutch laws on renting generally favor the tenant. If you engage a *makelaar* to act on your behalf, they will be aware of your rights and will explain them to you. Do not discuss the rental agreement with your landlord without your *makelaar* present. Verbal agreements are legally binding, and there are unscrupulous landlords, as there are anywhere, who will take advantage of your lack of knowledge. Generally speaking, read the fine print, and if you are at all unsure ask for expert advice before signing anything. If you want to know more, www.expatica.com has some useful information.

## APPLIANCES

Dutch plugs are two-pronged and use 220 volts and 50 hertz. If you are American, it is not worth bringing electrical equipment with you, as you will need to use transformers. British equipment can be used with normal adapters. American televisions cannot be used because they operate on a different system. If you have a multisystem video recorder, you can use it, but not one that is only a PAL system. American DVDs are also incompatible with European players. Normal home computers require expensive transformers, but laptops are especially adapted to be able to operate in Europe. Generally, it makes far more sense to buy locally and to sell when you leave.

## IDENTITY

The Dutch do not have identity cards, but you as a visitor will need identification. If you are staying for less than three months, you do not need a visa to enter from America or from other European countries. All you need is a valid passport.

If you are intending to stay for longer than three months, you will need to register with the Aliens Police (*Vreemdelingingenpolitie*), even if you come from within the EU. In order to register, you should go personally to the office, which is usually situated in the local police station. You may also have to be registered on the Population Register (*Bevolkingsregister*) at the Town Hall (*Stadhuis*) before you register with the Aliens Police. Check with the information office at the Town Hall or police station if you are not sure where to go. To register for work you need to obtain a work permit (*werkvergunning*) unless you are an EU citizen. You also need to apply for a SoFi, or Social Fiscal number, in order to pay tax and national insurance.

All registrations involve a lot of bureaucracy and you need to be patient. However, if you do not register life will become impossible because you cannot function in Dutch society without the necessary documentation.

**DAILY LIFE AND ROUTINES**
The Dutch get up at about 6:30 to 7:30 a.m., and the family usually has breakfast together before going their separate ways to work and school. On weekends, people may stay in bed for a bit longer but most are up and about by 9:00 a.m. If you stay in a Dutch home, it would be polite to join the family for breakfast. You will please your hosts if you make an effort to fit in and adapt yourself to their routines, so as not to cause them too much

inconvenience. Ask what *they* normally do. Some Dutch families attend church on Sunday, and you can decide what you want to do instead if you do not want to join them.

Breakfast normally consists of bread with a choice of ham, cheese, boiled egg, jams, or other sweet toppings, and perhaps yogurt. There may be cereals. You will be offered tea, coffee, milk, or fruit juice. Most people set off for work between 7:00 and 8:00 a.m. Schools begin at 8:15 or 8:30 a.m.

Lunch is a light meal, with a simple cheese or meat sandwich and soup, or fried eggs, ham, and bread. To drink there is fruit juice, milk, water, tea, coffee, or beer. Some children go home for lunch; some take a packed lunch to school.

When children come home at around 3:30 p.m., they generally have a light snack. Many then take part in sporting or other extracurricular activities. Of course, the older ones, from about the age of nine, also have homework.

Early evening is the time for the main family meal, usually served between 5:30 and 6:00 p.m. This is the main meal of the day and it normally consists of meat, potatoes, and vegetables, although foreign foods such as pizza, pasta, rice dishes, or noodles are also popular. Do not telephone Dutch people at this time! It will be considered a nuisance, and you will be dealt with rather curtly, or ignored altogether and left to speak to an answering machine. If visitors are invited, the evening meal may start a bit later. There are the same drinks as at lunchtime, although wine may also be offered. People generally go to bed between 10:30 and 11:30 p.m. during the week, and later on weekends.

## ATTITUDES TO CHILDREN

Children are encouraged to be social. They attend many organized activities, and often belong to sports clubs or other youth groups. They play together after school in each other's houses, in designated play areas, or on the streets. If the playing gets rough, adults tend not to intervene unless they have to. It is up to the children to sort out disputes for themselves. "*Je moet leren om voor jezelf op te komen.*" ("You have to learn how to stand up for yourself!")

Some Dutch children seem overindulged and unruly to American and British people. Children often address their parents by their first names from an early age, and their parents' attitude toward them can seem rather too relaxed to outsiders. Generally the Dutch like their children to make their own choices about how they conduct their lives. However, they do lead by example and ensure that their children are clear on what their values are. In this way, gentle pressure is exerted to conform—it is not turned into a confrontation. Dutch parents prefer to keep their children within the family fold, and if this entails a bit of compromise, so be it.

## SCHOOLS AND SCHOOLING

Education is free up to the age of sixteen (after that there is a minimal contribution), and Dutch schools are funded by the state, even though many of them are private or religious. We have seen that for years social and religious harmony was maintained in the Netherlands by the system of "pillarization." Groups from different sections of the community educated their children separately. Even today this is evident—Catholic, Protestant, Liberal (nondenominational), Socialist, Jewish, Islamic, and Hindu schools all exist. They are all obliged to teach the same curriculum, but the emphasis on the values of the school and the way that the religious calendar is observed will vary.

Most Dutch children start the *basisschool* (elementary or primary school) at the age of four, although attendance is not compulsory until they are five years old. They attend secondary school from the age of twelve to sixteen, seventeen, or eighteen, depending upon which direction they want to take for future employment. The different types of education are usually provided in the same building so that it is possible to transfer from one to another if the need arises. The exceptions to this are the *gymnasia*, which cater only to the most academic children. If a child attending a *gymnasium* consistently fails to make the grade, they will have to move schools.

All children at secondary school take the same subjects for the first three years and within that time it will be decided which type of education they will follow. The first type, MAVO, is a prevocational education and they leave school at sixteen. Then they have to attend further education classes related to their chosen field of work for a number of days per week until the age of eighteen. The second type of education, HAVO, prepares children to enter higher professional education and enables them to leave school at seventeen. Again, it is required for their employer to send them to college for so many days each week to complete work-related qualifications until they are eighteen. The third type of education, VWO, prepares the children to enter university, although they may choose to enroll in higher professional education courses instead.

Children who are more suited to practical work can attend VBO education, which lasts for four years and gives them a basic secondary education and the chance to learn practical skills. Children who have learning difficulties or other special needs can attend schools that cater specifically to their needs and that are designed to enable them to reach their potential in a caring environment.

### Public Knowledge

When young people have passed their diploma examinations—whether at the age of sixteen, seventeen, or eighteen—their parents will treat them to a party. If they have been successful, a school bag will be hung on the flagpole outside the house for the whole community to see their result. This can seem a bit harsh for those children who haven't passed, but if the bag is not there people know to commiserate and give encouragement for the future, rather than question the child on whether or not they have passed.

There are fourteen Dutch universities and many colleges of higher education. These are financed by the state, but higher education is not free and students (or their parents) have to contribute. Many young people live at home while studying at university or higher education colleges because accommodation is scarce and costs are high. Until recently, it was possible to obtain only two levels of qualification at a Dutch university. The first level of study lasted for four years and resulted in a qualification on a similar level to a master's degree, giving the title *doctorandus* ("Drs" is often seen on Dutch business cards). The second level led to the equivalent of a PhD and was designed for the best students. This two-tier system has recently changed to try to bring the Dutch more in line with the American and British systems, and it is now possible to get a bachelor's degree. Graduating from university is another special occasion for Dutch students and is celebrated by the family, as well as with friends.

## TV AND RADIO

Dutch noncommercial TV is funded from TV license fees. The Dutch Broadcasting Association (*De Nederlandse Omroep Stichting*) is an umbrella organization that coordinates broadcasting on the national television and radio network. On the three non-commercial television channels, airtime and funding are apportioned among the eight TV

networks based on, following the parliamentary model, the number of subscriptions they have. Radio airtime is divided up in a similar manner. The original idea behind the system was to ensure that the population was exposed to a variety of ideas, as each broadcasting company had a different ideology. It is now argued that it is becoming difficult to detect any difference in the program content of the broadcasting companies. The *Evangelische Omroep* (EO) is regarded as an exception as it still promotes a definite religious message and specific values. The Dutch cable-TV system enables the viewing public to choose between programs from several other countries, including Britain, France, Germany, Belgium, Italy, America, and Turkey. It is also possible to tune into radio stations from abroad.

## RESOLVING COMPLAINTS

In the Netherlands complaints are normally resolved by talking things through. The main aim is to preserve harmony and to come to a mutually agreed solution. If anyone's behavior is causing a nuisance, the offender can expect someone from the community to come and discuss the matter with them. If the matter cannot be resolved after it has been discussed on a one-to-one basis, it will be referred to the relevant authority to deal with—the local residents' association, a local government office, or the police. The Dutch use regulations to try to get a balance between preserving the individual's right to freedom of expression and lifestyle, and the needs of the community as a whole. It is considered important to avoid outright confrontation when a friendly word will solve the problem.

**CHANGING LIFESTYLES**

Many outsiders perceive the Netherlands to be an increasingly permissive society, as it is often at the forefront of legal reform. Legalized prostitution, homosexual rights, the decriminalization of soft drugs, and legalized euthanasia are controversial matters that have stimulated great debate. However, these changes to the law do not affect the lives of the vast majority of Dutch people.

The greatest changes to the Dutch way of life have been caused by new technology and globalization. Technology has stimulated consumerism, and globalization has reduced the differences between the Netherlands and other countries. This process has very far to go, though, before Dutch society is dramatically altered.

Some areas of the country still adhere to strict religious beliefs and a very conservative way of life; others are home to people living alternative lifestyles. For the majority of the population, however, conformity is the order of the day, and keeping to the general norms and values in order to promote a peaceful society (*samenleving*) is still an essential part of the Dutch way of life.

# chapter six

# TIME OUT

The Dutch have a decent amount of leisure time. They work 35 to 37.5 hours a week, and have four or five weeks' vacation allowance a year. Overtime is not usual, and there is no pressure to stay at work beyond the normal contracted hours. Many people accumulate extra days to enable them to take the occasional long vacation, such as to the Netherlands Antilles, where they can enjoy Caribbean sun, sea, and sand in an oddly familiar setting. Those restricted to school vacations travel in Europe or stay in the Netherlands—they may rent a house in the country, or go sailing on the lakes or around the waterways.

The Dutch are very fit and active outdoors. There are marked routes and opportunities to go walking, jogging, cycling, roller-skating, or roller-blading. Ask at a local tourist office (the VVV) or at an ANWB (motoring association) shop for booklets with the routes for your area. There are often designated picnic areas along the way, or you can take a break at one of the many cafés.

## SHOPPING

Shops in the Netherlands are called *winkels*, pronounced variously by the Dutch. To shop is *winkelen*, which means browsing around clothes shops and the like, or *boodschappen*, which means to shop for necessities. The process of *winkelen* is a leisurely affair, often carried out in one of the larger towns. Most of the shop assistants in the larger central stores speak English.

The Dutch do their *boodschappen* quickly and efficiently in local shops. They enjoy cooking with fresh ingredients, and tend to shop every other day for fresh produce and once or twice a week for general items. The joy of food shopping in the Netherlands is the abundance of specialty shops, usually of excellent quality. Some sell *biologische* (organically produced) food, which is more expensive. If you go into a small shop, you should wish the shop assistant and the other customers a "Good day" (see Chapter 9, Communicating). The staff in smaller shops do not always speak English, although they are normally happy to work out what you want.

The *bakkerij* (bakery) sells fresh bread and rolls, pastries, cookies, cakes, and sometimes homemade chocolates. The *slagerij* (butcher) sells fresh and cooked meat and some sausages. The *visverkoper* (fishmonger) sells fresh fish and some cooked fish to eat as a finger-food snack (not like British fish and chips). The *groenteboer* (greengrocer) sells fresh fruit and vegetables. A *kruidenwinkel* (herb shop) has herbal teas and other drinks, remedies, toiletries, and natural foodstuffs. A *drogisterij* (chemist) sells general products such as over-the-counter medicines (often including homeopathic remedies), hygiene products, and cosmetics. The *apotheek* (pharmacy) is a separate shop for the sale of medicines and the dispensing of prescriptions. Pharmacies have weekend hours to ensure that prescriptions can be collected in an emergency.

Many towns have at least one weekly market (*markt*), where you can buy a variety of goods for a set price—no haggling. Some larger towns have a separate flower market each week. Every so often, there is also a *rommelmarkt* (flea market), where

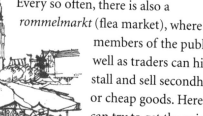

members of the public as well as traders can hire a stall and sell secondhand or cheap goods. Here you can try to get the price down. It is all an accepted part of the fun. You can find out the date, time, and place of any markets by asking at the VVV (tourist information center), the Town Hall information office, or by checking the local newspapers. Better still, ask a Dutch neighbor or friend.

When out shopping, you may be surprised by the normally polite and friendly Dutch. Be prepared to hold your own, or you run the risk of being jostled out of the way and ignored. Some shops (including post offices and banks) have a ticket dispenser, so that your ticket number determines the order in which you are served. If there isn't a ticket system, lines tend to be rather loosely formed and can come from two directions at once. Or there is a huddle, and the shop assistant will ask, "*Wie is nu aan de beurt?*" ("Whose turn is it next?") When it is your turn, stick up for yourself politely and firmly, or you will still be standing there half an hour later. This fits in with the Dutch view that everybody has to stand up for their own rights and not depend on others to do it for them.

### Shopping Times

The shops generally close between 5:00 and 6:00 p.m. on a Saturday evening and do not open again until 12:00 noon or 1:00 p.m. on Monday afternoon. There are exceptions: some bigger stores, supermarkets, and garden centers open on Monday morning. Once a week, usually Thursday or Friday, there is *koopavond* (evening shopping).

Check this locally. On *koopavond* small shops may close for an hour's meal break at about 5:30 or 6:00 p.m., then open up again.

The main supermarkets stay open on weekdays and Saturdays until around 8:00 p.m., but are also closed on Sundays. Some gas stations are open twenty-four hours, but usually only a few on the main highways. In the larger towns, the shops and garden centers are allowed to open by law for a limited number of Sundays each year. Check in the local press—the Sunday openings are well advertised. Just before Christmas the shops are allowed to stay open for longer hours. In Amsterdam the shops stay open for seven days a week until 10:00 p.m. and in tourist areas shopping hours tend to be longer.

**Flowers**

Flowers (including tulips, in a fantastic variety of colors) are cheap to buy and are beautifully arranged and presented in the shops. No town is without a large number of florists.

Selling tulip bulbs is big business, and the Dutch also export a significant volume of cut flowers. The horticultural industry holds a national exhibition called *Floriade* every ten years in a different area of the Netherlands. This is open to the public and is a great attraction for anybody who is keen on flowers and plants. The displays at Keukenhof each year show a wealth of spring flowers, including, of course, the tulip.

*A Dutch Icon*
Apart from the thousands of brightly colored clogs for sale in all the tourist shops, wooden clogs are still regarded as useful for certain activities. They are sturdy, and keep the feet clear of mud, and are most likely nowadays to be found on farms, or on sale in local garden centers.

## Mind Your Purse!

As is the case in other large cities in Europe, foreigners are seen as easy game by petty criminals. Keep your wits about you and be wary of anybody who approaches you in the street and tries to engage you in conversation, perhaps asking to borrow a mobile phone, or asking for money. It is best to reply with a firm but pleasant "No, sorry," and to walk on, ignoring any further requests. Generally such people do not make a continued nuisance of themselves after they have been firmly but politely rebuffed.

## BANKS

Banks are open on Monday from 1:00 to 4:00 or 5:00 p.m., from Tuesday to Friday from 9:00 a.m. to 4:00 or 5:00 p.m. and sometimes later on late shopping evenings. They are not open on Saturdays and Sundays. You will find ATMs called *geldautomaten* outside nearly all banks. They usually accept Maestro, Cirrus, Eurocard, Mastercard, Visa, American Express, and Plus Systems. You will also see *Chipknip* machines at the banks. These load a smart card with small amounts of money to reduce the need to carry cash.

The Netherlands is now part of the Eurozone and the euro has replaced the Dutch guilder. You can open an account with one of the main banks—for example the Rabo, SNS, ABN AMRO, or ING bank—or with the *Postbank* in the Post Office. The Dutch pay for purchases in shops either with cash (*contant*) or with a "PIN" code debit card—these have replaced the use of checks. Credit cards can be used for larger purchases, but are not accepted in all shops, so ask first. The Dutch mainly prefer to pay with money that they already have, and will save up for a purchase rather than use a credit card.

Bills are usually paid from the checking account (*rekening courant*). Standing instructions (*automatische overschrijvingen*) can be arranged for regular payments such as rent and club subscriptions, and direct debits (*machtigingen voor automatische overschrijvingen*) can be set up for gas, electricity, etc. If somebody comes to your home to provide a delivery, repair, or cleaning service they usually expect to be paid in cash, so make sure that you enough on hand. They will also expect to be offered a cup of coffee! People working for you over a period of time—for example, builders—will present you with a bill with their account number and ask for the money to be transferred into their account. This is done with an o*verschrijvingsformulier,* a transfer slip.

Currency can be changed in large hotels, and at banks, post offices, *bureaux de change* and at GWK (*Grenswisselkantoren,* literally "border exchange offices"). The official exchange rates at the GWK are often the best, and these offices can be found in most medium-sized and large railway stations.

## EATING OUT

Interest in other cultures and the multicultural nature of the Netherlands is reflected in the wonderful choice of food. Most large towns have restaurants offering cuisine from all over the world at different levels of price and sophistication. Generally, the Dutch dress casually when going out for a meal, unless it is for a special occasion at an expensive restaurant. The menu is displayed outside, so you can gauge the price and choice before you go in. Most of the larger restaurants have at least one menu in English.

There are also restaurants that double up as cafés (*Eetcafés*) serving Dutch-style food. These are usually clean, reasonably priced, simple and pleasant, with good fresh food and friendly service. They often start the day as a café, serving coffee and apple tart (*appelgebak*) in the morning, and then offer a simple menu for lunch—sandwiches, soup, *uitsmijter* (fried eggs, ham, and cheese served on bread), salads, and hot or cold drinks. Later in the afternoon (from about 5:00 or 5:30 p.m.) the menu changes, and it is possible to get a cooked meal of good-quality fresh produce with a decent choice of local or regional dishes. Dutch food is generally fairly plain—meat, chicken, or fish with fresh vegetables. Soups (try *erwtensoep*, pea soup)

and hearty stews are popular. The main purpose of eating is to gain energy for work and cycling, although of course the Dutch enjoy eating out for a change of cuisine and location as much as anyone else. Note that many small cafés and restaurants are closed on Mondays.

### Warning
Don't go into a "coffee shop" and expect coffee and Dutch apple tart. Under the Dutch "blind eye" soft drugs policy, "coffee shops" can sell customers up to five grams of cannabis for personal use. Unless that is what you are looking for, go to a café, a snack bar, or a department store restaurant instead.

If you want a snack rather than a meal, there are many options. Snack bars serve food that is quick and easy to eat, and often have high tables that you stand at. The idea is to eat and move on quickly. Such places normally sell *patat* or *friet* (fries, or chips), which you will be offered with *frietsaus* (mayonnaise) or *pinda saus* (spicy Indonesian peanut sauce). If you want ketchup, you will probably have to ask for it. You can also get *kroketten,* a soft meat-based filling, covered in breadcrumbs and fried, which is eaten dipped in mustard. They are extremely hot inside, so treat them with caution. The taste is also an acquired one. *Bitterballen* are similar in taste but shaped differently, *nasiballen* are fried rice balls, and *loempias* are Chinese fried spring rolls. If you are feeling brave, a typical Dutch dish is raw herring, which you hold by the tail, dip in diced raw onion, dangle over your mouth and bite. Not for the fainthearted, but a real Dutch experience! Another special snack that you may come across being made on stands in the street, often at festivals or fairs, is *poffertjes*. These are mini-pancakes (silver-dollar pancakes), which are made on a hot griddle while you watch. You could also visit one of the many Indonesian or Chinese restaurants where you can sit down to a meal, or collect a meal from the take-out (*afhaalcentrum*).

A good choice for a cheap Dutch meal in a relaxed environment is a visit to a *pannekoekhuis*, where you can buy pancakes (*pannekoeken*) with an amazing choice of fillings, savory and sweet. These are usually in holiday areas—often in the countryside—and they are a big hit with children.

**Toilets**

Toilets in a restaurant or café are usually free for customers. If you just pop in because you are desperate, you may have to pay—ask at the bar. Most department stores have toilets near the restaurant or café. These cost a few cents, which you give to the attendant on the way in, or leave in a dish on the way out. By the way, if you go to the toilet in somebody's house when visiting, be sure to leave it as clean and tidy as you found it.

## DRINK

The main drinks consumed by the Dutch are coffee, beer, and wine. The Dutch favor strong, filtered coffee, and drink a vast amount of it. They are also known for their beer: Heineken is a Dutch brew, a large amount of which is exported to America. Dutch beers vary in taste and strength. There are *wit bier* (blonde beers, which are cloudy), lagers, strong dark beers, fruit flavored beers, and seasonal beers, plus imported beers from other countries. A wide range of wines from all over the world can be bought in local supermarkets and wine merchants. The Dutch sometimes drink wine with their evening meal, at festive occasions, or just to relax and unwind in the evening.

You can try traditional Dutch alcoholic drinks, such as *jenever* (Dutch gin) and *advocaat* (eggnog). *Jenever* was originally used for

medicinal purposes. Now it is drunk ice-cold
from a shot glass filled to the brim, sometimes
with a chaser of lager. Ladies usually drink
*advocaat,* for example at a birthday party, after the
coffee has been cleared away. It is made from
brandy, egg yolks, and other ingredients and is
very sweet. It is served in a liqueur glass, but
people eat it from the glass using a small spoon,
rather than drink it.

*Proost*! (pronounced "proast" or "prorst")
means "Cheers!" in Dutch. Dutch people enjoy
drinking, but do so in moderation, and you are
not expected to become drunk, objectionable,
and *ongezellig.* Light snacks (*borrelhapjes*) are
normally served with drinks to soak up the
alcohol and enable people to have a good time
without becoming inebriated. The penalties for
drinking and driving are severe, and people will
not encourage you to drink when they know that
you have to drive afterward.

The most popular nonalcoholic drinks are
fruit juices, bottled water, iced tea, and milk. You
might try a *koffie verkeerd,* which
translates literally as "wrong
coffee," because it tastes like a
café latte and is considered
far too milky by most Dutch
people to be regarded as
proper coffee.

## RESTAURANT ETIQUETTE

When you go into a café you can usually sit where you want, although you will be expected to pick a table that is appropriate to your number. Some larger cafés have smoking and nonsmoking areas, but smaller ones do not. In a more expensive restaurant, you should wait to be shown to a table. Once seated, you will be offered a drink from the menu, then left to choose your meal, which you can order when your drink arrives. When your food is brought, you will be wished "*Eet smakelijk!*"—"Enjoy your meal!" You can reply "*Bedankt*"—"Thank you." If a person who is also about to eat says "*Eet smakelijk!*" to you, reply "*Smakelijk eten!*" To call a waiter say "*Pardon, meneer*" (or "*ober*"), or a waitress ("*Pardon, juffrouw*" (or "*mevrouw*").

Eating with your fingers is generally frowned upon—you will even be given a knife and fork with a sandwich—and so is cutting up your food and then eating it with just a fork. When you have finished eating, lay your knife and fork together to one side of the plate (positioned at 4:20).

The staff will usually ask you if you are enjoying your meal. If you are, you can say that it is "*Heel lekker!*" ("Very tasty!") If you have a complaint, try to resolve it with the waitress or waiter before calling for the owner or manager. Be polite and pleasant. The Dutch do not respond well to raised voices, and are likely to become distant and uncooperative rather than helpful.

Many more people smoke in cafés in the Netherlands than in America or Britain, so be prepared for this. You can ask to be moved to another table if it annoys you, but it is just as likely that the problem will be the same there. If you make a fuss, you will not be regarded sympathetically—in the Netherlands smoking is not an issue in restaurants, although it is becoming one in the workplace. You may also see dogs in restaurants. This is quite normal and is not considered to be particularly unhygienic. As long as the dogs are well behaved, and they usually are, they are tolerated.

To ask for your bill, say "*Mag ik de rekening alstublieft?*" If you need a receipt to claim business expenses, you can ask for one—"*Mag ik de kassabon hebben?*" or "*Mag ik bewijs van betaling?*"

### TIPPING
You do not need to tip in snack bars. In cafés most customers just round up the change. In restaurants you can give a tip for good service of 5 to 10 percent, unless it is already included in the bill. Many Dutch people do not tip at all unless the service is exceptional.

## SEX IN THE CITY

Dutch attitudes to sex are supposedly liberal and relaxed—everybody knows about Amsterdam's red light district. True, prostitution is legal in the Netherlands, but this stems from pure pragmatism rather than a liberal attitude. The feeling is that prostitution is inevitable, so it must be properly regulated, primarily to protect both customers and prostitutes, but also to ensure that the associated income is taxed. If you want to visit the red light district, you will be perfectly safe—it has the highest police presence in the city. Just watch out for the usual pickpockets. Women are unlikely to be harassed, but it is probably better not to go at night. Do not try to take photographs of the prostitutes.

Amsterdam is also famous as the Gay Capital of Europe. There are many gay and lesbian bars, clubs, and restaurants, and the city is at the heart of the Gay Pride week every June. Gay tourists flock to the city and the resident gay community is large—some figures put it at between 20 and 30 percent of the population in Amsterdam. The legal age of consent for homosexual sex has been the same as for heterosexuals since the 1970s, and since 1998 same-sex marriages have been legalized. Again, do not assume that the law necessarily reflects the views of the general public. Although homosexuals are protected from discrimination by the law, attitudes to them differ from place to place. While many university towns have a gay community, people in provincial towns are not as accepting of overtly gay or lesbian behavior as they are in the main cities.

## LEISURE

There are many leisure activities to choose from in the Netherlands, both indoors and out. You can find out about these at the *Vereniging voor Vreemdelingenverkeer*, or VVV, the local tourist information office, which has leaflets and booklets on local activities and activities further afield. You can also pick up useful information in the ANWB (the motoring association) shop, at the Town Hall information office, or in the local press.

In addition to the main festivals, many towns also have their own festivals. These can be good fun and give an insight into the local culture. Ask at the VVV office for details, or check out the Dutch Tourist Board's Web site. For children there are also local *kinderboerderij* (children's farms), theme parks, and many good zoos.

## HIGH CULTURE

The Dutch love of cultural activity goes hand in hand with civic pride and their belief in access for all. This is reflected in the number of theaters and concert halls around the country where classical music, opera, ballet, and plays are performed on a regular basis. The Royal Concertgebouw Orchestra and the Netherlands Philharmonic of Amsterdam are world renowned, as are the three main ballet companies—the Netherlands Dance Theater, Het Nationale Ballet, and the Scapino Ballet of Rotterdam. There is also the Netherlands Opera Foundation, which performs in the Muziektheater in Amsterdam. It is possible to book tickets for performances at the theaters and concert halls box offices, through the VVV, or through special reservation booking offices.

Check local papers for information about what is on in your area and read the *Roundabout* magazine for news of cultural activities in the major cities. You can get a season ticket for many theaters and concert halls, entitling you to advance bookings and to some discounts. Recitals are also held in many churches on weekends, and tickets can be bought at the door on the day of the performance. There are also small art-house cinemas.

The Dutch set great store by their cultural heritage and their history, and all self-respecting towns have at least one museum. There are also permanent outdoor exhibitions, for example, the

*Openluchtmuseum* (open air) in Arnhem, the Zaanse Schans windmill village, and part of the Zuiderzee Museum. Some of the places that are called *musea* (museums) are art galleries. You can buy a *museumjaarkaartje* that is valid for a year and gives free access to over four hundred museums and galleries throughout the country, including many of the main ones. The investment will pay for itself after a few visits. There is so much to see and do that you will be spoiled for choice.

## POPULAR CULTURE

Many of the theaters catering to audiences who enjoy the "high arts" also cater to those who enjoy more popular entertainment. There are

 musicals, lighter plays, comedies, reviews, and cabarets. Large towns have a mainstream cinema, usually with several screens inside. Around Christmas time, traveling circuses come to town. They perform in theaters or in big tents set up on the outskirts of the town. No section of the community is neglected and there is entertainment for people of all ages and tastes.

## COUNTRYSIDE PURSUITS

The Dutch go to the countryside as often as they can. Boating and sailing are common pastimes, and people flock to the lakes and waterways for rowing, canoeing, or speedboating events, or else they belong to sailing clubs. You can go on a canal tour (*grachtenrondvaart*) to see parts of the countryside and the towns from a different perspective. Horseback riding is popular and there are riding schools where you can arrange treks. Look in the Yellow Pages (*Gouden Gids*) under "*ruiterschool*" or "*manege*" for details.

There are several national parks in the Netherlands that offer the chance to see the fauna and flora of different types of natural habitat. Try a visit to Zwanenwater, Meijendel Nature Reserve, Brabantse Biesbosch Nature Reserve, or the Hoge Veluwe National Park. All the parks have marked paths and a visitors' center. The Hoge Veluwe National Park is also the location of the Kröller-Müller Museum, which houses a large collection of Van Gogh paintings. You could also visit Keukenhof—the famous flower park. It is open from late March to mid May, and again (for the *Zomerfest*, summer festival) from mid August to mid September.

The Dutch do not just use their bicycles for getting around during the week. It is common to see families cycling in the countryside on

weekends, or cycling clubs out in force to enjoy
one of the *fietsroutes* (cycling routes). Many
people also go hiking or walking in the
countryside. If you decide to do the same, make
sure that you stick to the *Wandelterreinen*
(designated walking areas), because certain parts
of the countryside are protected nature reserves.
Check with the VVV office for specified routes, or
have a look in the booklet entitled *Er-op-Uit!*
Produced by the Dutch Railway (NS) each year,
this gives ideas for day-trips to towns, attractions,
museums, and zoos. It also includes cycling,
walking, and roller-skating (in-line skating)
routes that start and end at railway
stations. The guide is in
Dutch, so you will have
to get someone to
translate it for you,
or better still keep
you company.

## SPORT

The Dutch like to be healthy and exercise
regularly. They enjoy participating in sport, rather
than just watching it on television, and generally
consider it to be worth the time and effort. They
are recognized on the international sports scene
for their prowess in soccer, rowing, speed skating,

hockey, tennis, volleyball, and cycling. They also like fitness training, walking, swimming, sailing, horse riding, and skating. There are clubs for baseball and softball, and auto racing is followed with enthusiasm.

One key winter sporting event that attracts a huge amount of attention and excitement is the *Elfstedentocht* (Eleven City Tour). This is a speed-skating event through Friesland that can only take place occasionally—when the temperature is low enough for all the canals along the route to freeze to sufficient depth. When the conditions are right, there is great excitement. A limit is placed on the number of participants and the route is lined with enthusiastic spectators. Anybody who cannot get there tunes in to the event on television.

# chapter seven

# TRAVELING

What strikes visitors first is the vast number
of bicycles, ridden by people of all ages. This
is the most popular form of transport in the
Netherlands. The next most notable feature is the
efficiency of the public transport system.

## CYCLING

People cycle everywhere, and use a car only for
longer distances. Most people have a bicycle, which
means that there are literally millions of them
about. You will be amazed at how many people can
fit on to one bicycle.

Children learn to cycle from an early age. They
cycle to school with one of their parents when they
are young, or in groups of students when they are
nearing the end of elementary or primary school.
It is not uncommon for secondary school pupils to
cycle nearly ten miles (sixteen kilometers) to
school and back each day, whatever the weather.

If you want to try cycling for yourself, this is
the ideal place for it. You can rent a bicycle for the

## NOTES FOR CYCLISTS

- **Obey the rules of the road.**
  These apply to cyclists as much as to other forms of transport. Cycle tracks have their own traffic lights and signs. Where there are cycle tracks, use them. You are not allowed to cycle on the sidewalk, as it presents a danger to pedestrians.

- **Lock up your bike.**
  Thousands of bikes are stolen, as it is a lucrative trade. Buy a secondhand one. It will attract less attention than a sparkling new one. Buy a good solid lock for it and never leave it unlocked, even for five minutes. If you buy a valuable new bike, get it insured.

- **Keep dry.**
  Buy yourself a waterproof jacket and trousers, and be prepared to dress in layers. It rains a great deal in the Netherlands.

- **Maintain the bike.**
  Make sure that the bike is in reasonable condition before you ride it and take a repair kit in case of emergency. You must have a functioning headlight, rear light, and bell.

- **Don't drink.**
  It is a criminal offense to ride a bike when you are over the limit for drinking (over 0.5 blood alcohol level).

day at many railway stations or from the larger cycle shops, or buy a secondhand one very cheaply. Many of the rented bikes are fairly basic and have back-pedaling brakes. If you are not used to cycling you could pose a danger to other people, who will assume that you can ride as well as they can. If you feel a bit unsure of yourself, practice cycling around a park a few times before you take to the roads.

## WALKING

The Dutch don't like walking just to get from A to B, or in order to carry out their daily business. They are far more likely to cycle or use public transportation. However, as we have seen, walking is a popular way to keep fit and many people walk for pleasure, either around the towns or in the countryside. As in any country, hitchhiking is risky and is rarely done in the Netherlands.

For the more adventurous visitor, there are special organized hikes across the tidal mud flats (*wadlopen*, walking across the mud flats). These endurance activities take place between May and October in the north of the country. They are good fun if you are fit and healthy, and do not mind being covered in mud and soaked to the skin; however, it is *essential* to go in a group with an experienced, registered guide.

## PUBLIC TRANSPORTATION

Public transportation is of a very high standard, although you might not think so if you listened to the Dutch complaining about it! In Britain people are delighted if a train is only a couple of minutes late, whereas the Dutch complain about the lateness of their trains as if the whole of Dutch society were disintegrating. They are used to an excellent level of service and rely on it, so they naturally become impatient and critical if any problems arise.

The Dutch railway system, called the *Nederlandse Spoorwegen* (NS), offers a convenient alternative to driving. It is only two hours by train from Amsterdam to the northernmost part of the country, and only two and a half hours to the southernmost part. If you are in a hurry, check that you are not getting onto a *stoptrein*, as these stop at all the small stations and take far longer to get between main towns and cities than the *sneltreinen* (high-speed trains) or intercity trains do.

You can buy tickets at automatic dispensing machines, once you get the hang of how to use them (ask somebody to show you), or at the ticket booth. You can buy single, return, and weekend return tickets. Children under four travel free but cannot occupy a seat. Children between the ages of four and eleven can get a very cheap "railrunner" fare when accompanied by an adult. There are many kinds of special discounted tickets.

Get a ticket before you board the train, or the conductor will charge you nearly double the fare.

If you take a pet with you on the train you will be charged according to its size and the distance of the journey. You can also take your bicycle on the train. A fold-up bike can be taken for free, as long as you have actually folded it. Normal bikes have to be paid for. Ask at the ticket booth.

## LOCAL TRANSPORTATION—BUSES, TRAMS, AND METROS

The buses usually link up with the railway timetable to provide an integrated transportation network. Buses perform a useful function for regional travel, and, along with the trams and metros, they provide transport in the cities and towns. The buses run from 6:00 a.m. to 11:30 p.m. To use a bus, tram, or the metro (in Amsterdam or Rotterdam) you need to buy a *strippenkaart.*

The country is divided up into zones and you have to use a certain number of strips per zone. When you start your journey you have to stamp the card in the machines in the buses, on the trams, and in the entrance halls to the metros. Drivers will expect you to have purchased your ticket before you board the bus or tram. You can buy a *strippenkaart* from the VVV tourist office, newsdealers, stations, post offices, and supermarkets. If an inspector finds you without a valid ticket, you will be fined.

## CAR AND DRIVING LICENSES

You have to be at least eighteen years old to drive in the Netherlands, and twenty-one years or over with at least a year's driving experience to rent a car. Tourists can drive in the Netherlands with a valid license from the United States or from Britain. You need to have held your license for longer than six months, and a normal license will need to be supplemented with an International Driver's License, which can be obtained from the Automobile Association. The law in the Netherlands requires you to have third-party liability insurance. If you actually have comprehensive coverage, you must get proof of this from your insurer. This is known as a Green Card.

## ROAD SENSE IN THE NETHERLANDS

- Driving is on the right side of the road.

- Speed limits are 30 km/h (18.5 mph) in residential areas, 50 km/h (31 mph) in towns and cities, 80 km/h (50 mph) on secondary roads, 100 km/h (62 mph) on highways as they go through city areas, with a top speed limit of 120 km/ph (74.5 mph) on expressways. Observe the limits.

- Speed cameras are being used increasingly to improve traffic control. If you are caught speeding, either you will be fined on the spot, or you will receive a bill in the mail. Pay promptly— the cost goes up the longer you leave it. If you have been speeding in an area where road repairs are being carried out, you can be fined up to 50 percent more than the normal rate for endangering the lives of the workmen.

- Familiarize yourself with the highway code and road signs.

- If you are on a road that is larger than the roads feeding on to it, you usually have the right of way. You will see marks like dragon's teeth across roads where traffic has to give way. At unmarked junctions or junctions between roads of equal size, traffic coming from the right has the right of way. If in doubt, slow down or stop, but look in your mirror first to ensure that a car is not going to run into the back of you.

- You are required by law to carry a warning triangle in case of accident and to use headlamp converters. It is recommended (but not compulsory) that you also have spare headlight bulbs, a first-aid kit, and a fire extinguisher in the car. You also need to have your car documents on hand in case you have an accident.

- In the event of a minor accident, you will need to exchange your car-rental details (if applicable), insurance details, and registration number, plus your name and address, with any other drivers involved. If somebody is injured in a car accident, you are legally required to notify the police. The emergency number is 112.

- Be extremely careful of cyclists. They do not always obey the rules of the road, but if you hit them, you are liable for damages. Give them plenty of space and be prepared for the unexpected.

- Roundabouts (traffic circles) are increasingly used as traffic-controlling devices. They are dangerous because many people seem unsure of the right of way. If there are dragon-teeth markings on the roads feeding into the circle, then traffic already on it has the right of way. Not everyone realizes this, so be cautious.

If there are *no* teeth markings, then you have to give way to the traffic coming on to the roundabout from the right at every road feeding on to it. Also, watch out for cyclists. The cyclists on the cycle tracks going around usually have the right of way. Even if they don't, they behave as if they do; it is better to go along with this than to kill or injure somebody.

- When turning right, be aware that there may be a cycle track going past you on the inside.

- Late at night some traffic lights are switched over to flashing amber, rather than working through red, amber, and green. This is to stop you having to wait at the lights when there is no traffic about. Approach the junction cautiously and note from the teeth marks on the road whether or not you have the right of way. There is a greater risk at nighttime of people driving recklessly due to alcohol or drug abuse.

- Seat belts are required for all passengers. Children under three must travel in the rear of the car in an appropriate safety seat. Children age three to twelve may travel in the front if they are in a special safety seat, but only if there is no room in the back. It is illegal to use a mobile telephone while driving.

- If you are in a city that has trams, be aware that they always have the right of way.

If you become a resident in the Netherlands and have a valid driving license that was issued in another country more than six months before your arrival, you can use it for up to 185 days (six months). You must ensure that you have either taken a test to acquire a Dutch license, or exchanged your own foreign license for a Dutch one within the six months. If you do have to exchange your license it is not a quick process, so allow yourself at least four weeks. Do not leave it until the end of the six months. If you drive after the six months is up and you still do not have a Dutch license you will be uninsured, which is illegal. You will also be uninsured while your application is being processed, so do not drive then either. This is a good time to try out the public transportation system!

The licensing requirements differ according to your country of origin, and there are some exceptions to the general rules. If you are in doubt about your own situation ask for advice at your country's embassy.

## Parking

There are plenty of multistory parking garages. Usually you take a ticket and pay at a machine on your way back to the car. There are also some parking meters. The traffic police keep a sharp eye out for people who stay longer than allowed, and you will be fined if you do so. Occasionally in spring they come and leave a tulip tucked under your windshield wiper with a note to say that you have parked well—a bit of positive reinforcement!

### Drinking and Driving

Drinking and driving is a criminal offense in the Netherlands if you are over the 0.5 blood/alcohol level. This applies to driving a car and to riding a motorbike, scooter, moped, or bicycle. You can be fined heavily. If your blood/alcohol level is over 1.8 your case will be taken to court and you may be banned from driving for a period of time, as well as being fined.

### TAXIS

Taxis can be hailed in the street in some of the main cities. However, in most towns and cities it is necessary to order a cab by phone. Look up the number in the *Gouden Gids* (Yellow Pages) under "taxis." You can also pick up one at a taxi stand.

*Treintaxis* (train taxis) are also available. You can buy a ticket for these if you are going to travel somewhere by train and know that you will need a taxi at the other end. The advantage here is that they are cheaper because you share them with other customers. You can buy the ticket when you get your train ticket or you can pay the taxi driver directly (although this is slightly more expensive). When you arrive at your destination, you look for the *treintaxi* stand (separate from normal taxis). *Treintaxis* operate within a defined area around the station—the area is shown on the taxi stand. You press the button and ask for a taxi to be sent to pick you up. When it arrives, it will wait for ten minutes to see if there are any other passengers, then the driver will work out the quickest way to drop you all off at your different destinations. For the return journey, you need to phone for the taxi half an hour before you need to be picked up.

## WHERE TO STAY

Accommodation is generally of a high standard. Whether you are staying in a city hotel or a *pension*, it will normally be clean and comfortable.

Hotels are rated on a one to five star basis, with five-star hotels as the top quality. The ratings are determined by the hotel's amenities rather than its ambience, and correspond fairly well with the equivalent rating in America or Britain, although the Dutch hotels are often smaller. Anything with a rating below one star is either a *pension* or a guesthouse. It is also possible to stay at hostels—there are certainly many of them in Amsterdam. There is an official Netherlands Youth Hostel Association. Their Web site is www.njhc.org if you want to make an inquiry.

The Dutch really enjoy camping and there are a large number of campsites that are also rated on a one to five star basis for their amenities and facilities. Some farms are also licensed to have a camping area. It is also possible to stay in self-catering *trekkershutten* (camping huts), which are more pleasant than their name indicates! These are likely to be near the coast, on the Waddenzee Islands in the north, or in wooded areas. Bed and breakfast establishments are less common than in America or Britain. It is possible to find them in resort areas, but in provincial towns they are almost nonexistent. Private homes can register at the VVV tourist offices as available to take guests but the standard of rooms is extremely variable.

Boat rental is another option for accommodation when traveling around the Netherlands. It is easy to arrange a boat rental. You do not need a *vaarbewijs* (boating license) for pleasure boats under 15 meters (49 feet), and that cannot go faster than 20 km/h (12.5 mph). The extensive network of waterways is easy to navigate once you have mastered the art of getting past the bridges and locks.

For more information on the great variety of accommodation available, go to a VVV tourist office or visit the ANWB shop. Both have books on sale that give full and up-to-date listings of different types of accommodation and their amenities. The VVV also has a booking service.

## HEALTH AND SECURITY

The Dutch health service is of a high standard. Members of the EU have a reciprocal health agreement entitling EU citizens to free medical advice and treatment. If you are British, take an E111 form with you. You will have to pay for nonemergency treatment and then reclaim it later. If you are not an EU resident, be sure to take out travel insurance with medical coverage. In case of emergency go to a hospital emergency department (*Eerste Hulp*), or dial 112 for an ambulance. For more information contact your embassy; ACCESS (www.euronet.nl/users/access) and www expatica.com also have useful information.

### Safety

The Netherlands is generally safe, with very little serious crime. Take the usual commonsense precautions that you would anywhere, particularly to avoid theft. Some of these have been mentioned earlier (see Chapter 6).

# chapter eight

# BUSINESS BRIEFING

## MAKING CONTACT

If you want to make business contacts, join
professional associations and attend the meetings
in your area, or go to courses or workshops, pop
into business *beurs* (fairs)
and talk to the people on
the stands. Make sure that
you always have good-
quality business cards
with you to hand out. It
is not acceptable to cold-
call people whom you do not know. Ask someone
to introduce you, or send an e-mail or letter to
introduce yourself and the topic, and say when
you will be getting in contact.

## OFFICE STYLE AND ETIQUETTE

Dutch business is egalitarian. Nobody is seen to
be more important than anybody else. Everybody
has their part to play in the success of an
organization, and this is acknowledged. Of course,

people know who the boss is, and respect senior staff, but the respect is two-way.

Do not be deceived by appearances. People may dress casually and use first names with each other, but there is focus on the business at hand, and that brings a slight formality. There is greater use of surnames and titles in dealing with unfamiliar business acquaintances.

**Working Practices**

Quiet efficiency is a hallmark of successful Dutch business. The total number of hours worked a week is restricted by EU employment law. Normal office hours in the Netherlands are generally from 8:00 a.m. to 5:30 p.m., Monday to Friday, with little or no office working on Saturday. Many people work flextime or part-time. Even some senior managers work part-time. Lunches are usually short (thirty to forty-five minutes), and taken in the office or in the staff cafeteria.

Once rules have been agreed upon, discipline is self-imposed rather than imposed from outside. The Dutch are keen on punctuality. If you have an appointment, do not be late. It is unlikely that you will be able to reschedule an appointment at the last minute, as people plan their time carefully and well in advance. There is a "closed door" office culture, primarily because time is at a premium and it is easier to work when undisturbed. The office environment is clean, well-ordered, and quiet. There is no rigid barrier between home and office, and people do sometimes take work home. They can be called there on an important matter, but prefer to keep their time at home free for family and friends. Do not assume that you will get a good reception if you disturb their evenings or weekend.

## WHO ARE DUTCH BUSINESSPEOPLE?

Like their German colleagues, Dutch businesspeople enter the job market later than their British and American counterparts. Education is important. As in Germany, there is a strong system of apprenticeship and on-the-job training. Key factors in promotion are education and qualifications, competence, hard work, ambition, and networking ability.

Today people working in all industries and organizations in the Netherlands have to be flexible. Contracts are often fixed-term, and it is not unusual for employees to move on to another company within three to five years. Flexible working patterns are the norm. Until recently, times were good economically, and this is reflected in the terms and conditions of employment. These include maternity/paternity rights, generous vacation allowances, and sickness benefits, which are now regarded as standard. However, "fringe benefits" such as company cars are rarely part of the basic employment contract. People may get bonuses for their performance, but they are not guaranteed long-term employment or a comfortable retirement.

Dutch egalitarianism and a sense of social responsibility mean that women have equality in the workplace—in theory at least. In practice there are few women at board level. Until recently, many women did not return to work after having children. Over the past decade the situation has changed, and women now make up about 35 percent of the workforce. Many work part-time, often job-sharing.

## COMMUNICATION STYLES

The Dutch are noted for their outspokenness. They tell you what they think concisely, and without frills. This can come across as abrupt, rude, or even arrogant, to other nationalities. On the whole, exchanges are conducted with openness and without rancor. While the Dutch will tell you their views, they are also open to hearing your ideas. They expect professional people to be well informed and to have opinions on economic, business, and political matters. Do not get drawn into a discussion if you do not know what you are talking about: they will be disappointed in you, and unimpressed.

Foreigners sometimes mistakenly assume that the direct, relaxed, and egalitarian business culture of the Dutch implies an informal environment. The Dutch are in fact quite focused and formal and expect the conventions of business to be adhered to. When you are first introduced to somebody, take your cue from them. If the person wants to be addressed by their professional title or surname, they will use it to introduce themselves. If they are formal, so should you be until invited to use first names.

The Netherlands used to be a "write first, then speak" culture. This has changed with the pace of business, but first-time contact is normally by letter or e-mail, followed up by a phone call.

Letter-writing is a formal affair and there are standard conventions for business letters. The Dutch are particular about getting professional titles and forms of address correct. If you are unsure about what title to use, find out before you send the letter. If you get it wrong, you could cause offense. When giving your own job title, include your university degrees, because higher education is valued in the Netherlands, but be warned! A bachelor's degree is *not* highly regarded. Put only master's degrees and above.

Traditionally all verbal agreements used to be

followed up in writing, but the pace of modern business does not always allow for this. However, an e-mail confirming the points agreed upon in a telephone conversation never goes amiss.

Theirs is a concise culture. The Dutch like simple, clear information, and to get to the point quickly. Telephone conversations tend to be short and voicemails are commonly used for messages, which are usually returned or acted upon quickly. Always give your name clearly at the start of a telephone conversation.

## PRESENTATIONS

The Dutch expect detailed technical presentations, supported by relevant facts and data. A sincere, "soft-selling" approach is important: they distrust high-pressure, high-enthusiasm presentation styles, although they may enjoy the show. An hour-long presentation is acceptable, and they may stop you to ask for clarification. Make sure that you leave plenty of time for this.

The Dutch expect to enter into direct and vigorous debate; outspoken questioning is a sign of interest rather than antagonism. They may interrupt you, and your interrupting them will not cause offense. Frankness and openness are the watchwords of discussion, and it is important that you express your views clearly. Any "beating around the bush" may be perceived as deviousness, and if you try to bluff, your bluff will be called. It is important not to speculate, and you will gain more respect for being open about limitations and constraints. If you mean "no," say "no," and do not give tentative answers. Don't make any promises that you can't keep.

Subjective feelings or emotions have no place in a business discussion, and are regarded as inimical to clear, rational, decision-making. Flowery language, flattery, and rhetoric are regarded as false and suspect. Irony, sarcasm, and jokes that mock anybody else are not appreciated, though you can make a joke at your own expense.

You should be well-informed, well-prepared, and to-the-point. Information should be presented in a positive manner, but without exaggeration.. The Dutch will give you their full attention and make notes for future reference. You should do the same. Do not leave issues unresolved. They consider it important for the advantages and disadvantages of a new product, proposal, or service to be stated, and they expect to be given transcripts, brochures, and copies of any data presented. They look for price, quality, and delivery of service, and discussion of these must be included in a presentation.

The Dutch generally do not go in for small talk within business meetings, but will happily talk about more general matters over lunch or dinner. Most Dutch people have a strong sense of social justice and social democracy, and may react adversely to right-wing views. Be careful not to sound superior about your own or your country's achievements, and do not criticize the Dutch, even if you seem to be being invited to do so.

## TEAMWORK

If you are running a Dutch team, or working with one, what can you expect? In the Netherlands a team is a group of individuals united for greater efficiency and profit under a strong leader, chosen for specific technical competencies. To work well they each need a clear understanding of their responsibilities and authority.

Consultation is a key feature. Although the team leader's decision is final there must be consultation on all key issues. This can take a great deal of time and outsiders can regard the process as irritatingly long. However, there is no rushing it along. The Dutch set great store on giving everybody the right to express their opinion and make a contribution. Once a decision has been reached, action will be taken and the necessary paperwork completed. However, you occasionally find that people who have disagreed with the outcome may not cooperate or put any effort into making it work.

Dutch team members expect competence, reliability, and a rational approach to problem-solving from their leader. They appreciate sincerity and constructive criticism. They react badly to pretentiousness and flippancy. Do not treat them lightly, or ignore details.

## LEADERSHIP AND DECISION MAKING

A Dutch senior manager will have experience and expertise, as well as a good standard of education. Managers see themselves as "first among equals" and are encouraged to cultivate a straightforward style. It is expected that a decision will be reached only when all the parties concerned have conducted a full analysis. The manager takes responsibility for the success or failure of the project, and the final indicator of success will almost always be financial profitability.

Dutch managers tend to avoid status symbols such as large expense accounts and a big car, as extravagance is frowned upon. As befits an egalitarian ethos, it is important for them to be prepared to listen to all levels of the company.

Even where there is a vertical hierarchy there is no problem about "going over someone's head" to get information. Younger organizations have a matrix hierarchy to ease communication.

A good Dutch manager will come across as confident, friendly, energetic, and ready to "get his or her hands dirty." Questions should be answered frankly and directly and should not be avoided. Willingness to debate and to listen to subordinates is prized, even though this inevitably slows down the decision making. Managers are expected to be well organized, to deal in facts, not sentiment, and to set clear objectives and targets.

Taking advantage of one's superior position, making decisions unilaterally without consultation, intolerance, and attacking another's position without justification are all ways of losing employees' and colleagues' respect.

## MEETINGS AND NEGOTIATIONS

Dutch meetings are mainly for making decisions and clarifying procedures. There will be a clear timetable and an agenda, which will be adhered to. Dress may be formal or informal, but the quality of the clothing will be uniformly good. People may take off their jackets during a meeting (as in Britain, it is a sign of getting down to work)—follow the lead of the Dutch people present. Seating is

normally informal, with the presenter or leader of
the meeting at the "flipchart" end of the table.

The pace of the meeting will be steady. The aims
and objectives will have been clearly stated and the
atmosphere will be reasonably serious. Technical
issues will be presented in sufficient detail to enable
full consideration, and participants will be expected
to bring with them (and to have read) all the
relevant documents. However, do not assume that
steady deliberation means total transparency. The
Dutch are past masters at negotiation. Their aims
are to get a favorable deal, with long-term profit,
and to establish long-term relationships. They may
put pressure on you to make decisions, and they
will not be above bluffing about their own aims in
order to find out your true objectives. They expect
to debate plans with you in detail, and distrust
intuition unsupported by facts. However, they are
open to innovation, and if terms are clearly laid out
they are willing to compromise.

## HANDLING DISAGREEMENTS

When there are disagreements, you may be
surprised by the outspokenness of your Dutch
colleagues. They prefer to express disagreement
honestly, and to resolve matters by logical
argument. This means that you should be
prepared for a long and intense debate and to

support everything you say with facts and data. Be as honest as you can, and respect others' right to disagree. It is important to speak up about disagreement. Silence may be seen as tacit acceptance. Also, avoid expressions such as "I can tell you in confidence" or "between you and me." This goes against the Dutch spirit of openness.

## *GEZELLIGHEID* AT WORK

The concept of *gezelligheid* extends beyond the social sphere into the work environment. If you are visiting a company in the Netherlands, you may well find that you are expected to join in with colleagues on social occasions such as birthdays or retirement parties. You may also be invited to participate in office outings.

Brian is a fairly reserved English manager. Whenever he visited the Netherlands for his work with a Dutch company, he was invited to join in any social event that was taking place. Being the quiet type, Brian far preferred a peaceful meal on his own at the hotel and an early night. After a few visits to the Netherlands, he noticed that the people in the office were not as cooperative and friendly as they had been at the start of his association with them. This puzzled him, and he asked one of his Dutch colleagues what had gone wrong. His colleague explained that the team members thought he wasn't interested in them because he constantly turned down invitations to take part in their activities. As a result, they were no longer interested in him.

# chapter nine

# COMMUNICATING

**LANGUAGE**

Dutch is spoken in the Netherlands, and Flemish is spoken in parts of Belgium and the northwest of France. There is very little difference between the two—about the same as between American, British, and Australian English. Frisian, a minority Germanic language, is spoken in the northwestern province of Friesland.

Many Dutch people speak excellent English (it is the main foreign language taught in schools). It is often difficult to practice speaking Dutch, because so many people reply to you in English, but try at least to learn the basics, for occasions when it would be polite to use it. People may respond with a slight smile because your pronunciation sounds rather quaint to them. Do not be put off by this. They will be pleased that you have made the effort. Many people also speak good German and French.

You may find that some English words regarded as offensive in America and Britain are used freely in the Netherlands without the same connotation. (Don't be surprised, for example, if you hear young children saying "Shit!" It is used more as an exclamation than a swearword, and is not intended to be offensive.)

## FAMILIAR AND POLITE FORMS OF ADDRESS

The Dutch have different words both for the singular and plural pronoun "you" and for the formal and informal "you." The informal you is "*je*" (plural "*jullie*"), and the formal is "*u*"(both singular and plural). When addressing older people, or if you are in a formal context, it is better to use the "*u*" form until you are invited to switch to "*je*." Err on the side of politeness rather than risk giving offense.

Up until fairly recently, "*je*" was used only for family and close friends but this has now changed and attitudes are far more relaxed. Generally speaking, you can use the "*je*" form to speak to people who are younger than you are, or around the same age. If you have already been invited to call someone by their first name, "*je*" is the correct form to use.

## GREETINGS IN SHOPS

Up until a few years ago it was customary for people working in shops to address customers as "*u*." However, younger people are so used to addressing everybody as "*je*" that this is now becoming widespread and acceptable. You will usually be greeted in a shop with "*Goede morgen*," "*Goede middag*," or "*Goeden avond*," or good morning, afternoon, or evening. If you can cope with trying out the gutteral "*g*" sound, it is best to reply in kind. If not, then reply pleasantly in English. This prompts the sales personnel in many shops to switch to English to put you at ease.

When you have completed your purchase, the salesperson will say good-bye and may well wish you a good day. "*Dag*" (or "*tot ziens*) *meneer/mevrouw en een prettige dag* (or *avond*) *verder*"—"Good-bye" (or "until the next time") sir/madam and enjoy the rest of your day (or evening)." You can reply "*Dag*" or "*tot ziens*." If someone has taken the time and trouble to help you to find something, you can say "*Bedankt voor de moeite*," which means "Thank you for making a special effort to help me."

## WRITTEN COMMUNICATIONS

Written Dutch is far more formal than spoken, and invitations and business letters (especially to customers) can appear very formal by comparison with American and British practice. They often include rather ornate set phrases that are considered the polite way to express matters on paper. When the Dutch send e-mails to people they have not met they use the same principles as for business letters, and so even e-mails are very formal, although they are much shorter than letters. If e-mails are being sent to somebody who is known to the sender, they are generally short and to the point, and no space is wasted on niceties. This is intended to be direct and to save time—after all time is money.

## TELEPHONE SYSTEM

The telephone system in the Netherlands is run primarily by KPN-Telecom, although it is now possible to use other companies and costs have been driven down. The country code for the Netherlands is 31 and each area of the country has its own local code.

You can dial anywhere directly from public telephones in the Netherlands. Within the country dial 0 and the area code, from overseas dial 00 31 and the area code without the 0. To dial out of the Netherlands, dial 00 before the country code number—for example 00 44 for Britain. For directory inquiries for numbers within the Netherlands, dial 0900 8008. For overseas directory inquiries, dial 0900 8418. You can use the local phone book for residential numbers, or the *Gouden Gids* (Yellow Pages) for business numbers.

Coin-operated public telephones are being phased out and replaced by card-operated telephones, but coin-operated ones remain at some railway stations. You can use your credit card to pay, but it is generally more convenient to buy a phone card. Some post offices also have public telephones.

When a Dutch person answers the telephone, they give their name, for example, "*Met Yvonne van der Gouw*," literally, "with Yvonne van der Gouw." They will be somewhat taken aback if you do not answer your telephone in the same way. Just saying "Hello" is considered rude and unhelpful. Generally speaking it is not advisable to call people after 10:00 p.m. Even if they are not actually in bed, they are likely to be winding down and will not appreciate the disturbance.

## POSTAL SYSTEM

Post offices (PTT) are open Monday to Friday from 8:30 a.m. to 5:00 p.m., and on Saturday from 8:30 a.m. to 12 noon or 1:00 p.m. Most of the staff in post offices speak good English and are happy to help and advise you. Stamps (*postzegels*) can also be purchased in many newsdealers, souvenir shops, and tobacconists. Mail boxes are red and can be found on streets and outside post offices. Local mail goes into one slot and the rest into the other (*Overige Postcodes,* Other Postal Codes). Mail is delivered to Dutch houses once a day, normally in the morning, except for Mondays.

If you have a remote access e-mail account (for example, Hotmail) you can use an Internet café, paying a time-based charge.

## MISINTERPRETATIONS

The Dutch soften the tone of what they are saying with small words such as *toch* (yet, still, for all that, all the same), *even* (just), or *een beetje* (a little). Unfortunately, when they are speaking in English these subtle modifications are not always translated and it can make them sound rather overbearing and bossy. They may say the sentence correctly in English, but it comes over as *too* direct and forceful. The Dutch are certainly not shy about giving their opinion, but when speaking English they can sometimes sound as if they are insisting that you do things their way, rather than making a suggestion. This can lead native English-speakers to misinterpret what is being said to them and the manner in which it is being said, and to take offense when none has been intended.

Generally, business people who are used to speaking English for work convey the essence of the meaning in English, even if their grammar and pronunciation are a bit off the mark. Some Dutch people who think that they understand English very well may misinterpret what you are trying to say to them. You can usually tell this by their response, as they have evidently "got hold of the wrong end of the stick," and it is necessary diplomatically to rephrase what you are saying.

Occasionally, people translate a Dutch proverb directly into English and expect you to understand what they mean. Some proverbs are very similar—for example, "The straw that broke the camel's back" is "The drop of water that made the bucket overflow"—but this is not always the case. Many Dutch proverbs have to do with farming or the sea, and do not make sense until they have been explained to you.

## HUMOR

Judging from the popularity of English-language sitcoms on Dutch and cable television, you would think that the Dutch sense of humor is very similar to the American or British. In some respects it is. The Dutch like to poke fun at the establishment and they also appreciate humor that involves wordplay, repartee, and mimicry. Popular cabaret acts are often based upon this approach, with some bawdiness and slapstick thrown in for good measure. In fact, much of the humor is based upon teasing and bringing people into line, reflecting the "*Doe maar gewoon . . .*" principle—letting people know their faults in a lighthearted way and ensuring that they do not take themselves too seriously. If you are on the receiving end of the teasing you are expected to take it in good humor.

## CONVERSATION

Very few topics of conversation are taboo. Perhaps the only one that is off-limits entirely is how much people earn or the value of their possessions. The Dutch enjoy conversation over glasses of beer or countless cups of coffee. The livelier it gets, the better. You can expect people to give their opinions on all sorts of matters—sex, politics, religion, the weather, the royal family, education, whatever has been on television the night before, or in the newspapers. They also like to discuss what is going on in their local community—what the neighbors are up to (making sure that it is noted that they are only commenting, not criticizing), what the local authority is doing in the area, which stores are opening or closing, and so on.

They are usually keen to find out what you think as well. At times, it becomes so boisterous that it is difficult to make yourself heard. People talk over each other loudly and interrupt because they are eager to get their own point of view across. To outsiders, this can seem rude and very heated, but do not worry. Once the conversation has ended everybody arranges to meet again for coffee and goes home good friends.

Be prepared to join in both the social chat and the serious discussions. Take the lead from your Dutch friends. If they feel comfortable with you they will broaden the conversation to include more topics. It is unusual to discuss personal difficulties in a group, and good friends will steer the conversation away from subjects they think may make you uncomfortable or distress you. (Personal issues are more commonly discussed on a one-to-one basis.) Conversely, you may find that total strangers, perhaps on the train, will ask you some extremely direct questions about current issues. This is because you will be regarded as representative of your country, and they will want to hear what you have to say about your own country's affairs or how you view theirs. You can be frank, but be prepared to support what you say with a good argument.

## BODY LANGUAGE
Dutch people are friendly, and will shake hands or give a light embrace when kissing cheeks in greeting, but otherwise they keep their distance

physically. It is not the norm to be physically demonstrative, so if you are the type of person who touches people as you are speaking to them, or gives them a bear hug when you arrive or leave, you may well get a cool response.

The Dutch are a straightforward lot; they look people in the eye and expect the same in return. If you don't do this, you will be regarded as shifty and untrustworthy.

In a business setting it is rare for people to use personal space or their environment to intimidate staff or colleagues, or to demonstrate their status. Most managers have a desk and a table in their office. If somebody comes to talk to them, they will usually come out from behind their desk and sit with the person at the table, so that they are on a more equal footing. Even at board meetings, there is rarely a set place for the chairperson to sit, and people just sit where they are comfortable. Your body language should show that you are relaxed and confident, and should not be used to put other people at a disadvantage.

Body language in the Netherlands is generally very similar to that in Britain, although it is possibly more reserved than in some areas of America. Whatever else you do, make sure that your handshake is firm and that your smile reaches your eyes!

## CONCLUSION

The Dutch are an admirable, complex people. Despite superficial similarities with modern American and British culture, they have a distinctly different take on the world, born of a proud tradition of self-reliance, fair dealing, and enterprise. In order to give a broad picture of Dutch society we have had to generalize—to explain what "normally" happens in particular situations. Of course, as with any society there are many subcultures. There are sections of Dutch society that live by traditional values. There are also groups who look outside the Netherlands for new ideas. The Internet and other communication networks have accelerated this process.

Today, the character of Dutch society is under threat from globalization and the creation of a homogeneous international culture. The Dutch may well rise to the occasion. Let us hope they do. Their traditions of fairness and social justice are important to the world. Their business acumen and practical commonsense benefit us all. A world without the Dutch sense of curiosity, zest for life, and unique balance of liberalism and conservatism would be a poorer place. The Netherlands offers the open-minded visitor a refreshing point of view, a lively cultural scene, and the real pleasure to be found in the company of its friendly and energetic people.

# Further Reading

Boucke, Laurie and Colin White. *The Undutchables—An Observation of the Netherlands: Its Culture and Inhabitants.* Colorado: White/Boucke Publishing, 1996.

De Rooi, Maarten (text), Frans Lemmens (most of the photography), and Tony Burret (transl.). *Visions of the Netherlands* (English version). Alphen aan de Rijn: Dutch Publishers, 2002.

Fuller, Mark (ed.). *Alphabet Soup—Decoding Terms in Dutch Business, Politics and Society.* Amsterdam/Antwerp: Business Contact/Het Financieel Dagblad, 2001.

Gazaleh-Weevers, Sheila. *Here's Holland.* Utrecht: Van Boekhven/Bosch, 2000.

Van der Horst, Han. *The Low Sky—Understanding the Dutch.* Sciedam: Scriptum, 2001.

Van der Horst, Han. *The Low Sky in Pictures.* Sciedam: Scriptum, 2001.

Vossestein, Jacob. *Dealing with the Dutch.* Amsterdam: Kit Publishers, 2001.

Zonneveld, P. A. W. van, and G. J. van Zonneveld (eds.). *A Curious Landscape.* Alphen aan de Rijn: Atrium, 2000.

*At Home In Holland.* The Hague: The American Women's Club of The Hague, 1998.

*The Holland Handbook.* The Hague: XPAT Media, 2003–2004 edition.

culture smart! netherlands

# Index

# Acknowledgment

I would like to say a big "thank you" to the family members and friends who have helped me compile this book—contributing ideas and tips, and giving encouragement and support.